'Celebrating Our Centenary'

The story of what God in Christ has done through the Anglican Church in West Nile
1918 - 2018

by
Christians of the Church of Uganda
Madi and West Nile Diocese

Copyright © 2018 Diocese of Madi and West Nile, Church of Uganda

Editor: John Haden

Photographs, maps and illustrations used by kind permission of the original owners, where traceable

First Edition 2018

All rights reserved

No part of this book may be reproduced or utilised in any form or by any means, electronic, or mechanical, including photocopying, recording or by any other information storage and retrieval system, without permission in writing from the publisher, the Diocese of Madi and West Nile, Church of Uganda.

ISBN: 978-1-912082-67-4

Unless otherwise stated, Scripture quotations in this publication are from the Holy Bible, New International Version, Copyright © 1973, 1978, 1984 International Bible Society.

Published by the Diocese of Madi and West Nile, Church of Uganda and by Barny Books in the UK
Printed in Uganda by The Print Shop, Kampala
and in the UK by Spiegl Press Limited, Stamford

Contents

Foreword by the Rt. Rev. Henry Luke Orombi 4

Acknowledgements by the Rt. Rev. Charles Collins Andaku 6

Chapter 1: 100 years of Anglican Church History in West Nile in decades Canon Isaac Jaffer Anguyo 7

Chapter 2: West Nile before and around the time the Gospel came Drani Ronald Bileah and Alioma Yosamu 10

Chapter 3: Planting the Seed - The Establishment of the Native Anglican Church in West Nile John Haden 18

Chapter 4: Watering the Seed - The work of missionaries in the growth of the Anglican Church John Haden and David Sharland 25

Chapter 5: The Growth of the Church in West Nile Various authors 54

Chapter 6: The Bishops of the Anglican Church in West Nile The Publicity Committee of Bishop Andaku's Consecration and Moses Aluonzi Alaka 83

Chapter 7: The Revival Movement in West Nile Enzama Wilson and Canon Ondoma John 108

Chapter 8: The Growth of Ministries within the Church Various authors 119

Chapter 9: Organisations Supporting the Growth of the Church in West Nile Various authors 133

Chapter 10: The Church and Education in Madi and West Nile Diocese Juliet Zilly Paratra 159

Chapter 11: The History of Health Services in West Nile Heather Sharland 162

Chapter 12: The Church and Socio-Economic Development Jackson Atria and Christopher Yiki Ondia 175

Chapter 13: The Church and Politics Harold E. Acemah 183

Chapter 14: The Most Difficult Times the Diocese Has Gone Through Canon Isaac Jaffer Anguyo 185

Appendix 1: List of Missionaries and Overseas Christians who worked with the Anglican Church in West Nile 190

Appendix 2: Ugandan Clergy ordained in Madi and West Nile Diocese and Nebbi Diocese 197

West Nile District at the time of Uganda's Independence in 1962 (from John Dobson's Book 'Daybreak in West Nile' with permission)

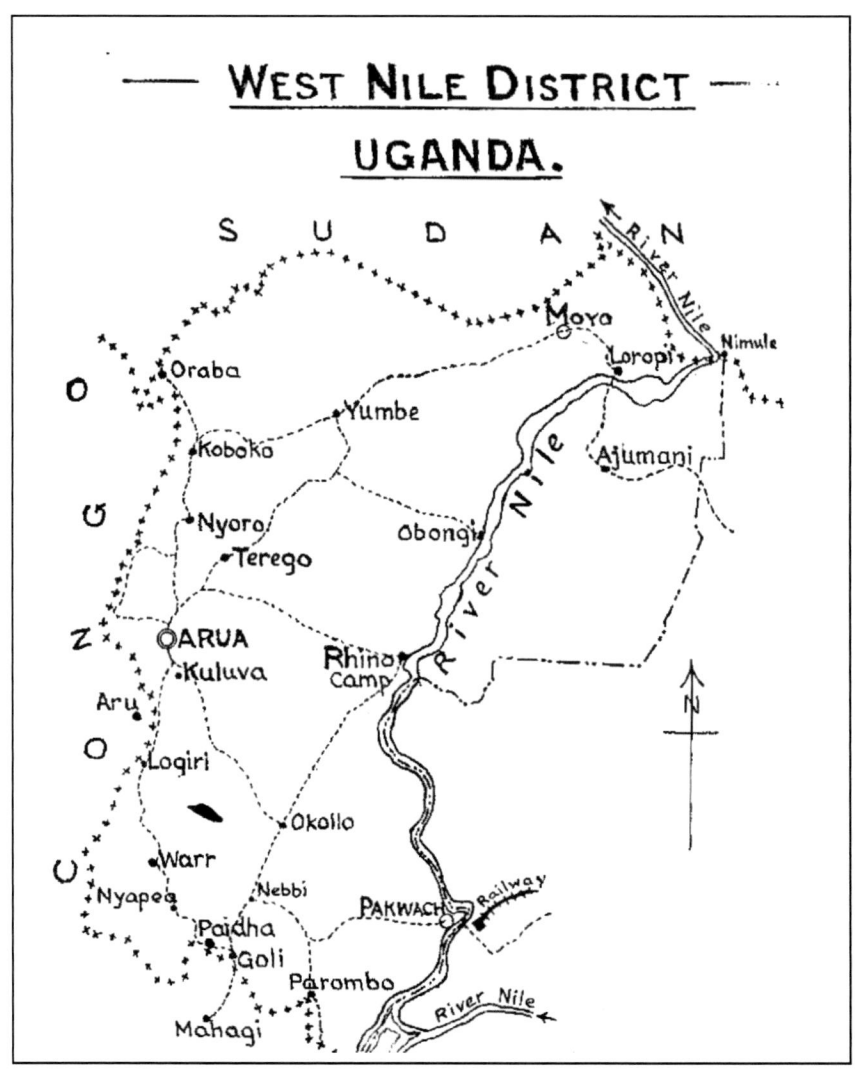

Foreword

The Diocese of Madi and West Nile, created in 1969 out of Northern Uganda, has been a home to many tribes, who have worked together since its creation. The joy of knowing this great gift of God for a united church will go back to the beginning. The missionaries, who came to evangelize this area, gave themselves sacrificially to walk with the West Nile people. The beginnings were difficult, travels were hard, health conditions were poor, but some of the people were receptive to the message of God.

Although at the beginning, things were slow, but later our people saw the value of education, health facilities and church governance. This was the message of the gospel, expressing the love of God through the missionaries. Their teaching, and willingness to dwell with the people, was an incarnation of the Gospel of Christ. Today, some still remember the early missionaries, and the ones who followed them, because many of them walked the talk.

As the church grew, in number and in faith, it was necessary to create a diocese west of the River Nile. This diocese became the first one in Northern Uganda to be created, to be followed much later by Lango and Kitgum. Then Madi and West Nile Diocese was able to create the Diocese of Nebbi.

The Bishops, who were called to lead Madi West Nile Diocese, were very committed to the spread of the word of God, so much so that the Anglican Church in West Nile is very sound biblically. Our Africa Inland Mission root has been a blessing, because that is how we have been brought up, to cherish the word of God.

As we read the story of what God in Christ has done through the Anglican Church in West Nile, we shall experience so much of the product of faithful sacrifices, of many who gave themselves to portray the love of God physically. One will notice the growth of the church in the number of men and women ministries, and of the young people movement which is one of the most active in the country. The influence of the church is strong in many areas, including both the ministries to families and in the numbers of schools, both Primary and Secondary. It is also commendable that the UGANDA CHRISTIAN UNIVERSITY, a church-founded institution, has a campus in Arua, the main centre in this region. It is the influence of the church here which has contributed to so much development.

Finally I must thank those who have been able to put together materials which will enable the younger generation see the journey of the church in West Nile. This is making us appreciate our history, because such knowledge makes you humble when you know how much others paid to make you who you are.

I want to thank the present bishop, Rt. Rev Collins Charles Andaku, for being the one to spearhead the writing of this Centenary Book, which was launched by his predecessor, Bishop Joel Obetia.

Please take this book and read it, and you will be more informed about Madi and West Nile as never before.

TO GOD BE THE GLORY.

Rt. Rev. Henry Luke Orombi
Former Archbishop of the Church of Uganda

ACKNOWLEDGEMENTS

The Planning Committee, which was selected by the Madi and West Nile Diocesan Synod, came up with five reasons for celebrating the 100 years of the work of the Anglican Church in West Nile. It is worth mentioning two of them:

The celebrations provide opportunities to take a **look back** to **rediscover how** the church came into being, its early ministry and how it has grown over the 100 years.

To **connect the stories of the lives** of those who helped to spread the gospel, and died in service in the last 100 years, with the future generations.

This book you are holding in your hands today has helped to achieve these two objectives. There is a common saying that, "It takes many to write a book." I sincerely thank all those who have submitted chapters; 25 people have done this. Thank you to all of you and to the people who gave photographs, did the editing, proof-reading, and organised the printing.

I wish I could thank each one of you by name, but allow me to mention a few who gave their time, resources and much more to help get the book to what it is today: John and Jenny Haden, they received the raw materials for each chapter, organised it and gave the book the flow it needed. Canon Isaac Jaffer Anguyo, besides his work as the Chairman of the Centenary celebrations, helped to get the chapters from the contributors, did some preliminary editing and sent them to Mr. Haden and Mrs Kathryn Asiku. Mr. David Sharland coordinated receiving a collection of photographs from different sources, including Betty and David Payne. The History and Documentation Committee headed by Rev. Canon Alfred Jeth Adiburu gave guidance to Mr. John Haden and Canon Isaac Jaffer Anguyo.

May the Glory go to our Lord God!

Rt. Rev. Charles Collins Andaku
Bishop Madi and West Nile Diocese.

Chapter 1: 100 years of Anglican Church History in West Nile in decades by Canon Isaac Jaffer Anguyo

Our book is the story of what God has done through the Church of Uganda Madi and West Nile Diocese. But before we tell that story, perhaps we should set it in the context of the wider history of Uganda.

1914-1919: Assumption of British rule; arrival of the Verona Fathers and African Inland Missionaries; AIM settling in Mvura, later called Mvara; the famine in West Nile; First World War

1920-1929: The first converts and African members of Native Anglican Church (NAC); movement of African Evangelists from Mvara to other parts of West Nile to plant NAC; the Vollors - longest serving AIM missionaries arrive

1930-1939: The African Evangelists (church planters/teachers) face challenges from the locals; Emmanuel church in Mvara is built

1940-1949: The second famine and the exodus of the people in the region to work in Buganda to pay taxes; Christians from West Nile started their churches in the Diaspora; resistance to formal education in many parts of the region including areas surrounding Arua and Mvara Mission; the East African Revival makes its way to West Nile; it faces opposition from the Missionaries and the Abalokole were heavily persecuted by the police; first local clergy ordained after training from Buwalasi in Mbale; the Maclures and other long serving missionaries arrive; Second World War

1950-59: Political campaigns as Uganda prepares for independence from the British; Parties formed along denominations - Uganda National Congress (UNC), Democratic Party (DP), Kabaka Yeka (did not have impact in West Nile); Lugbara Bible translation into advanced stages by Laura Barr who improved on the Lugbara orthography; Ringili established as Technical school and later developed to Theological Training Centre

1960-69: Uganda gains independence; the church also gains independence from missionary leadership, but missionaries remain in key positions; the Bible is translated into Lugbara; UPC and Kabaka Yeka fall apart; Obote assumes presidency; complete Lugbara Bible translation published; African Missionaries sent from West Nile to Karamoja; Madi and West Nile Diocese carved out of Northern Uganda with Bishop Silvanus Wani as its first bishop

1970-79: The most turbulent period in Uganda: frictions develop between the Acholi and the Langi; Obote is overthrown and Amin takes over; many from West Nile assume leadership roles especially in the Army; business Asians expelled from Uganda and businesses given to Africans, especially Muslims and Nubians; the economy of the country collapses; Janan Luwum is martyred and the church faces persecution; many leading Christians go into Exile; Bishop Silvanus Wani elected Archbishop; Bishop Remelia elected as the second Bishop of Madi and West Nile Diocese; Amin is overthrown; there is revenge killing in West Nile; huge exodus of people into exile in Sudan and DR Congo

1980-89: Rapid changes in the national leadership, including Obote coming back to power second time; armed opposition to Obote rule; economy not recovering; Obote is overthrown second time; Tito Okello comes to power and resistance to his power by National Resistance Army/Movement continues until his government is overthrown; Christian Rural Service (CRS) starts programmes in the Diocese; Hooyer, missionary, works with CRS; Bishop Remelia retires and is replaced by Bishop Ephraim Adrale as the third bishop; foundation stone of Emmanuel Cathedral laid by Bishop Ephraim; Mothers' Union introduced in the diocese by Salome Adrale; Archbishop Wani retires from office; Here is Life founded to work with the church in Aringa

1990-99: NRM under the leadership of Museveni consolidates its power; the economy begins to pick up; new Constitution is made for the country and elections are held; Bishop Adrale dies; Rev. Caleb Ariaka Nguma elected as the fourth bishop of the diocese; Nebbi Diocese carved out of Madi and West Nile Diocese with Bishop Henry Orombi as its first Bishop; Bishop Nguma serves for a short time and dies in motor accident; Bishop Wani serves as a caretaker bishop until Rev. Dr. Enock Drati is elected as the fifth Bishop; Bishop Wani dies in his home; very big division develops between Bishop Drati and Archdeacon Girism Draku; this becomes a big black mark in the diocese

2000-10: As the year 2000 approached, people thought a lot of bad things were going to happen including crashing of computers; even perhaps a good thing, the return of Jesus Christ; Bishop Henry Orombi becomes the Archbishop of Church of Uganda; UCU Arua Study Centre started at Ringili; Bishop Drati retires and Bishop Joel Obetia becomes the sixth bishop; he inherits the Drati-Draku problems; his first years in office are more of fire fighting with the lowest Diocesan income and resources

2010-   : Bishop Joel announces his retirement; Synod appoints a committee to plan the Centenary Celebrations of the Anglican Church in West Nile in 2018; Bishop Charles Collins Andaku is consecrated and enthroned as seventh Bishop of Madi and West Nile Diocese.

Life in West Nile in the 1920s and 1930s

Women carrying cotton
to the ginnery at Rhino Camp

Women grinding cassava on a rock at Mvara in the 1930s, where the new Cathedral now stands.

Chapter 2
West Nile before and around the time the Gospel came
by Drani Ronald Bileah and AliomaYosamu

Introduction
West Nile covers the area between the River Nile, as it flows out of Lake Albert and heads north towards South Sudan, and the Nile-Congo watershed along the range of hills west of the river. This area was known during colonial times and up to this day as West Nile. The present Arua District forms the largest portion of the area. The region is inhabited by a variety of ethnic groups of which the main ones are: Lugbara, Alur, Madi, Kakwa, and Kebu. They are small stateless societies who speak Sudanic and Nilotic languages, the kind of 'segmentary lineage' societies studied by generations of social anthropologists. West Nile is one of the most ethnically diverse parts of Uganda, the most significant groups being the Sudanic Lugbara, Nilo-Hamitic Kakwa, and Nilotic Alur.

Christianity has made a greater impact here than in other parts of Northern Uganda. Islam is also a significant force in Aringa County. Despite being such a 'multinational' region of Uganda and having being carved out by accidents of history and geography, the people live in harmony with one another.

The coming of the Arabs and Islam in West Nile
The roots of Islam in West Nile can be traced to the 17th century era of slave trading. According to one historian, it was the Sudanese Muslim soldiers who were employed by Khedive Ismail of Egypt who brought Islam to Northern Uganda, West Nile and some parts of Bunyoro as early as 1830s. The Egyptians and North Sudanese Arabs who invaded southern Sudan were slave traders. Their main route was along the Nile valley with Dufile as their transit centre. They entered West Nile from the north through Koboko, where they were said to have converted many locals to the Islamic religion before reaching Arua.

In the Aringa area, Islam is known to have been introduced by Fadhimula Adu who was appointed chief of Aringa by the British. Adu was taken as a slave into Sudan and later converted to Islam and moved to Mombasa and came into Uganda from Mombasa. When the British were looking for people who could interpret for them, Adu was appointed and in the process became chief. He used the opportunity to convert the Aringa to Islam.

The coming of Islam into most regions of Sub-Saharan Africa was through trade, carried along major trade routes which established Muslim commercial communities in the midst of local African societies. This was the case in West Nile, where alongside trading centres, mosques have been planted even if now they are without followers and called 'Bee-hives'.

Historians believe that Emin Pasha, employed by the Khedive of Egypt to take a military force up the Nile valley, recruited his troops from a combination of ethnic groups including the Nubians from the Sudan. Members of tribes like Acholi, Kakwa, Lugbara, Nyoro, and many others, adopted Nubi Islamic practices, their language 'Lunubi' (Kinubi), their dress and other cultural systems. The Nubi community today are mainly found on the northern side of Arua town and in Bombo, near Kampala.

In the 1860s, Muslim Arab slave traders came into West Nile to capture slaves and get ivory. These very brutal foreigners were led by Northern Sudanese and Egyptian Muslims claiming Arab descent. They burnt houses and raided villages with guns to capture people as slaves, killing, beating and torturing local people. They forced men and women to carry their goods, took the able-bodied to work for them or to sell for profit, while children and old people were left to die without help.

Since the societies in West Nile were without kings or chiefs, they suffered at the hands of the slave traders, known in West Nile as the Khartoumers, and in some areas called Tukutuku, because they came from the capital of Sudan called Khartoum. Those Africans who had close contact with Arab slave traders and who accepted Islam were able to live better lives as they were not subjected to this brutality.

As a result, most people in what is now West Nile came to associate both the Islamist religion and foreigners or outsiders with brutality, as their enemies. This had a great impact not only on Islam but also on the Christian church in West Nile. Many locals came to fear and reject foreigners and foreign religion, running away from foreigners and from any religious belief brought from outside. Christianity was often perceived as a European or Western religion, which played an essential role in promoting European civilization and despised traditions cherished by Africans.

Impact of Islam on Christianity
In Africa, Christianity and Islam have often been in competition for the soul of the Continent and this rivalry has sometimes resulted in conflict. This was true in West Nile as Christianity was introduced after Islam had already taken root in the region.

When the Native Anglican Church and Catholic churches were introduced by the white missionaries, many people in West Nile either became hostile or ran away from the European missionaries or completely avoided foreign religions. Both the Arabs and local African Muslims became hostile to the coming of the Christian Church to West Nile, which was seen as interfering with the spread of Islam in the area.

However, unlike the brutal Muslim slave and ivory traders, the early European missionaries, who came to establish Mission stations in West Nile, showed love and kindness. They helped the poor and sick, provided education and technical and modern agricultural training. This attracted local people to the Christian Church in West Nile. Despite Christianity being introduced late to this part of Uganda, it has made a greater impact here than in other parts of Northern Uganda.

Although there were religious conflicts between Muslims and Christians in the process of winning converts, the African tradition of tolerance moderated this hostility. Even in post-Independence Uganda, this tradition of religious tolerance moderated the competition between Christianity and Islam. Milton Obote, the protestant President of Uganda used to boast that his extended family in Lango consisted of Muslims, Catholics and Protestants 'at peace with each other'. Obote's successor, Idi Amin Dada (a Muslim), also had a similarly multi-religious extended family and even once declared that he planned to have at least one of his sons trained for the Christian priesthood.

However, for a while, the attitude of the people of West Nile as in other parts of Uganda wavered between the Cross and the Crescent. To them, the arguments of the advocates of each faith seemed almost equal.

Colonialism and the Birth of West Nile
West Nile was the last but one district to be added to Uganda, the last being Karamoja, which followed in 1922. Right from its inception in 1914, West Nile was a multi-ethnic district consisting of four ethnic groups, with the international boundaries of Uganda dividing them. The Lugbara, Kakwa and Alur were split between Uganda and Democratic Republic of Congo, and the Kakwa and Madi between Uganda and Sudan. Because of this, events in these neighbouring countries have had a direct impact on the people of West Nile.

Belgian Rule
Belgians were the first European colonialists to arrive in the Congo/Nile Watershed in 1885. Under the command of Van Kerckhoven, the Belgians pursued the remnants of Emin Pasha's forces up the Nile to Wadelai and eventually convinced them to join them at their headquarters at Wandi in the present Terego County in West Nile. Belgian control of the region was consolidated when their King Leopold II signed a treaty with the Zande chief Zamoyi. The Belgians defeated the Mahdist revolt at the battle of Rajaf in 1897, and established the Lado Enclave as part of the Belgian Congo Free State.

The Lado Enclave
West Nile was at that time part of this 'Lado Enclave', named after the river port of Lado on the Nile in the Sudan, and part of the Congo Free State. Following the Heligoland Treaty of 1890 and another of 1894, according to these treaties, the Belgian King Leopold II's control over the territory would cease when he died. Accordingly, in 1910, the Lado Enclave was transferred back again into the Sudan.

During the first decade of the 20th century in the scramble for territory in the Region, the British had tried to control the Sudan in order to secure the flow of the Nile. To achieve this, the boundaries between the Sudan and Uganda were adjusted so that Sudan ceded the southern tip of the Lado Enclave, the area of West Nile, to the Uganda Protectorate. Between 1912 and 1913, a joint commission of Anglo-Belgians mapped and agreed the Belgian Congo/Uganda Protectorate border from Lake Albert north-eastward to the Congo/Nile watershed. A Sudanese/Uganda commission also agreed the common boundary between Bahr al Jabal, the Belgian Congo and the Uganda Protectorate near the present Ariwara. The new boundaries were officially promulgated on 21st April 1914 by the British Government.

Accordingly, the British Secretary of State pronounced the area west of the River Nile, formerly a southern part of "Lado Enclave", part of the Uganda Protectorate and named it West Nile District. In return, the area east of the River Nile in the Nimule area, which had been part of the Uganda Protectorate, was transferred to the Anglo-Egyptian Sudan. On 3rd February 1915, the boundaries were officially recognized by the two colonial powers, the British and the Belgians. This process finally helped the British to control the Nile waters from the source up to Egypt.

British Rule
When, in 1914, the British established their Protectorate in West Nile, their first District Commissioner (DC) was Alfred Evelyn Weatherhead. He served from

1914 to 1922, assisted by Jack H. Driberg, who was also an academic analyst and anthropologist.

World War I 1914-1918
The First World War of 1914-1918 was a European war since its causes and most of the fighting took place in Europe. By then, Uganda and Kenya were under the British while Tanganyika, now Tanzania, was under German rule. The British wanted to recruit soldiers from West Nile to fight for them, but the Lugbara in West Nile looked at the British and Belgians with suspicion and discontent as enemies and elephant shooters for ivory. Most refused to join the British regiment, the King's African rifles (KAR), but some did volunteer for military service. In some cases, the British forced Africans to fight for them. However, things gradually improved when DC Weatherhead stopped elephant shooting for ivory and initiated development projects like roads and house construction. He used chiefs and law courts to keep peace, law and order. This reduced the West Nile's people's fear of the white men and foreigners.

The coming of Christianity to West Nile
The British colonial officials were soon followed by Christian Missionaries, both Catholic and Protestant. In West Nile, the Catholic White Fathers had travelled up the Nile and reached Lake Albert by 1910. They established a Catholic Mission near Arua in 1915. It was the African Inland Mission which established the first Native Anglican Church in West Nile in 1918, as described in the next Chapter. However, local people were not interested in Christianity. They regarded missionaries as foreigners and as agents of the colonial government, who were in many aspects against African traditional way of life. Although some people accepted Christian teaching and sent their children to the missions for baptism and education, many elders, especially among the Lugbara, at first openly cursed such people.

Reaction to Foreign Rule
In 1919, the people of West Nile reacted against the establishment of foreign rule. The *Allah Water or Yakanye* rebellion was inspired by the able leadership

of Rembe. They used Yakanye (water), which Europeans described as a hallucinogen and an aphrodisiac, a drug which changed previously timid men to brave warfare and violent opposition to British Imperial rule in West Nile. Ole'ba was the centre of Rembe's activities. The cult appeared to pose a real threat and the rebellion was ruthlessly dealt with by the British. Many local chiefs who were suspected of being associated with Yakanye were exiled to Ankole and Masindi until 1925. Rembe himself was caught and hanged.

Despite stiff resistance to the establishment of colonial rule in West Nile, the British overcame that resistance and introduced several political, religious, social and economic reforms. In 1925, the first professional labour recruiters arrived in Arua, laying the foundation for the first labour system in West Nile.

Economy
The economic potential of the "Lado Enclave" that had most attracted the Arabs and Europeans to the region included iron, ostrich feathers, ebony, timber, fibres, tamarind, gum, honey wax and rubber. On top of these, there existed numbers of elephants and white rhinos. These were highly valued commodities in Europe and Asia. The River Nile also provided opportunities for fishing and a transport system.

Famine
Famines during the early periods of colonialism in West Nile occurred in 1918, 1930, 1936, 1943 and 1946, with the most catastrophic in 1943. A recent study revealed that this famine could be attributed to locust invasion 'ombi', drought, army worms "kalute"; and "sima" or "Tukutuku" and "kuliabatu" invasions. According to the findings, the worst famine which hit the region led to many people starving to death. As a strategy to avert the economic crisis, people

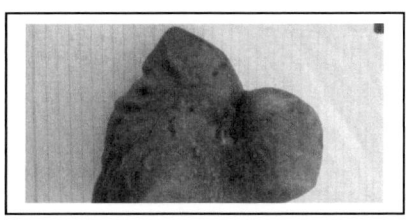
Wild yams eaten in famine

resorted to eating wild fruits, roots and grains, some of which were poisonous which killed several people. These included among others variety of wild yams ('obua', 'guruna', 'likieya', 'ebio') and 'sungu' or bambara nut.

Furthermore, people crossed international borders, especially between Uganda and Congo, in search of food. In the process, many women were reportedly raped by the Congolese soldiers before they were allowed to cross the border, a situation women had to tolerate because they wanted to save their families from starving to death. Children were exchanged for food items with one child to one 'agbaka' basket either of sorghum or millet as the standard measure.

A new policy of storage of food was introduced by the colonial government whereby food reserve was centrally instituted at every sub-county headquarter and each family was also encouraged to keep a portion of the harvest in order to avert a future food crisis. This came to be known as "miri anya" or public millet. Until recently, many communities in West Nile had granaries "ero" in which they stored food. This is fast disappearing, although there is still rampant food insecurity in the region

Today, the economy of the region is booming because of its strategic location in the heart of Africa, particularly bordering South Sudan and Democratic Republic of Congo (DRC). The region celebrated the centenary of colonial transfer from Belgian Congo to British Uganda in 2014. The government of Uganda has earmarked Arua Town to become a city in their Vision 2040 plans and many developmental projects are taking place in the proposed city. This has come with severe challenges for the Church as urbanization brings in a lot of evils such as crime, prostitution, corruption and religious conflicts. The Anglican Church needs to adopt measures to prepare their flock to meet the myriad of challenges of unemployment, education, Information Communication Technology (ICT), globalization, and the relationship between the Church and the State.

Chapter 3 Planting the Seed
The Establishment of the Native Anglican Church in West Nile
by John Haden

"I planted the seed, Apollos watered it, but God has been making it grow. So neither the one who plants nor the one who waters is anything, but only God, who makes things grow." (1 Corinthians 3:6-9 (NIV))

It was the Anglican Church, through the Church Missionary Society (CMS), who brought the Christian Gospel to Uganda and established Anglican Churches in every area except one. So how was it that today's Church of Uganda Diocese of Madi and West Nile, was actually founded not by the CMS but by another Mission, the Africa Inland Mission (AIM)? Just who and what was and is this Africa Inland Mission?

The Gospel came to West Nile during the First World War. Nearly four thousand miles to the north, the nations of Europe were grinding out the last twelve months of a war which had already nearly bled them to death. Before the start of the conflict, the land west of the River Nile and north of Lake Albert had been ceded by the Belgium Government to the British, to form part of the Uganda Protectorate. It had been part of the Belgian Congo and there was a Protestant Church already planted amongst the people living there, on the west side of the watershed between the Rivers Nile and Congo, the Lugbara, the Alur, the Kebu and the Kakwa. The new international north-south boundary cut right through their homelands.

The first Protestant Churches in the north-east of the Congo had been planted by missionaries from the Africa Inland Mission (AIM), an interdenominational faith mission, which had been started 17 years before by a young Presbyterian Minister, Peter Cameron Scott. He was born in Scotland, but went with his parents to Philadelphia in America, so he had both Scottish and American roots. He very nearly became a concert singer, before hearing the call of God to full-time Christian service. He accepted ordination and trained in a Philadelphia missionary college before being sent with his brother John to serve in West Africa. Within a year, John had died of black-water fever, the development of malaria which took so many missionary lives in the early days, and Peter Cameron Scott's missionary efforts had borne no fruit.

Sick and disillusioned, Scott returned first to London on his way home. He was taken by friends to Westminster Abbey where he had a profound experience of God's calling, while kneeling before David Livingstone's tomb. He believed that God was calling him to establish a chain of Christian churches from Mombasa on the Indian Ocean through East and Central Africa to the southern edge of the Sahara Desert in the region of Lake Chad. Within another year, he and friends in Philadelphia had established a Mission committed to working in East and Central Africa, to be both interdenominational and international, at that time both American and British. They decided to call it the Africa Inland Mission (AIM).

It was to operate under the faith mission principle, of not directly appealing to the public for funds, trusting that God would supply their needs. Scott led a small team to East Africa and they established the first AIM 'station' at Nzawi, inland from Mombasa amongst the Akamba people. But by December 1896, Peter Cameron Scott had died at Nzawi, after a brief attack of black-water fever; he was just 29.

In what was to become Kenya, AIM went on to establish a chain of Africa Inland Churches, a new denomination modelled on their own reformed Protestant theology. In the Belgian Congo, where they planted their first church at Kasengu in the hills above Lake Albert in 1912, AIM planted churches which now form the CECA 20 denomination, the Communauté Evangélique au Centre de l'Afrique. Meanwhile, in the British Protectorate of Uganda, the British insisted that just three faiths could operate, the Protestant Anglican Church of Uganda, the Roman Catholic Church and the faith of Islam. This meant that, in Uganda, all the other denominational missions like the Baptists, the Methodists and interdenominational missions like AIM, were not allowed to work or to plant churches.

In late 1917, a party of AIM missionaries was travelling up from Mombasa, through Uganda to join their colleagues in the Congo. They planned to work along the Congo side of the border amongst the Alur and Lugbara people. The party included were Americans, men and women. Walking up from the Nile valley towards Vurra on the Uganda/Congo border, one woman in the party became very ill. They stopped on the Uganda side of the border at the Government Rest Camp at Vurra to allow her to recover.

While they were waiting there, at Ezuku about eight miles from Arua and a mile from the Congo border, they heard from the first British District Commissioner in Arua. DC Alfred Weatherhead was struggling to deal with the effects of a major famine in West Nile. He asked the AIM group to help with the distribution of famine relief food. He had also asked the Catholic Fathers to help. The AIM party realized that the people to whom they felt called, the Lugbara and the Alur, were in fact the same people they were now being asked to help. They agreed to stay in West Nile provided that they could engage in missionary activity.

At that time, there was no Protestant church work in the area, because West Nile had been a part of the Congo. The Anglican Church Missionary Society had not yet been able to start work in the District although it had been made part of the Anglican Diocese of the Upper Nile. This vast Diocese, with a cathedral at Ngora near Soroti, covered most of Uganda north of the Nile and much of Southern Sudan, all under just one Bishop!

The AIM group asked the Church Missionary Society if they might start evangelism in the area. This was agreed by the leaders of the two Missions, with one stipulation. To preserve the unity of the Protestant Church in Uganda, the AIM group were asked to ensure that any church planted in West Nile would be part of what was then the Native Anglican Church. Ever since, Christian workers, from the United States of America, from the United Kingdom and now from many other countries, have always ensured that while working in West Nile, they supported the Anglican Church of Uganda.

In 1918, the small group waiting near Vurra were joined by experienced AIM missionaries from the Congo. Frank and Edith Gardner brought their baby daughter Beryl and Frank's brother, Alfred, across the border to start church-planting work in West Nile. The Gardners were from the Baptist Church at Chipping Norton in England and they already had a number of years of experience of working in Africa. Frank had gone with the Zambezi Industrial Mission as a missionary and worked in Nyasaland for five years, with his brother alongside him for most of that time. They were joined by Edith, a young shop-assistant from the same Baptist Church at home in England. The Gardners were married within days of her joining Frank.

When they returned to England for leave, they planned to return to Africa. But their Mission told them that there were no funds for their return journey. Rather than stay in England, they decided they would transfer to another Mission and were accepted by C T Studd's Heart of Africa Mission (HoAM), which was then working in the Congo. Frank and Edith were accepted by HoAM, travelled by sea to the mouth of the Congo River and inland to Leopoldville. By 2017, they had arrived in the area of the Belgian Congo inhabited by the Zande people, not far from where AIM had already planted a church at Dungu. After having had some difficulties with HoAM, the Gardners, Frank, Edith and by then baby Beryl, together with brother Alfred, met with the AIM team at Dungu and applied to join them and the AIM. This was agreed and the Gardners became members of AIM, the third Mission with which Frank had served in Africa.

But they were not at Dungu for long. Over in West Nile, Uganda, the AIM party had arrived at Vurra on their way up from the coast. Frank had been advised that he and Edith should move again as he had suffered two bouts of black-water fever. Although there was malaria in West Nile, the high, open area was thought to be healthier for him. So when the AIM Congo field conference at

Dungu learnt of the new opening offered in West Nile, they agreed that the Gardners, their new Baptist recruits with a wealth of missionary experience, should move across the border to lead the new work of planting Anglican churches in West Nile. God does indeed work in mysterious ways, British Baptists, serving with a Mission started by an American Presbyterian, were to plant the seed that would grow into an Anglican church!

The Memorial at Ezuku, which commemorates the first AIM Missionaries to work in West Nile: Frank and Edith Gardner, and Alfred Gardner, and some of their colleagues. It was erected by Rev. Canon Penina Enyaru, the first woman to be ordained and the priest of the Ovisoni Parish, in the 1990s.

While still at their Vurra base, the Gardners were told that Awudele the elder of the area had given land for them at a place called Mvara about a mile to the east of Arua town. For six days each week, the Gardner brothers cycled the ten miles from Vurra to the site of their new work. They first built a round hut for Alfred, and then a larger hut for Frank, Edith and their baby. These were simple structures, with openings for windows and a space for a doorway, but no actual doors or windows. Edith must have found the lack of privacy and the constant observation of the local people very difficult. Even worse was the challenge of digging wells while their neighbours did their best to spoil them, according to the notes she kept of the things that troubled her.

They cooked outside on three stones and lived very simply on rice and sweet potatoes. They used the camp beds they had brought with them and a cow-hide stretched across four stakes to sleep on. Their initial priorities were to complete a functioning well and then to start a worship service, giving access to fresh water and to living water. Having established the beginning of what was to become AIM's Mission Station at Mvara, Frank arranged for a small bungalow to be built in the shade of a large tree.

The painting of 'Our bungalow at Mvara', by Frank Gardner.
(Pictures of house and family below kindly provided by his grand-daughter, Mrs Rosemary Thomas.)

They began to use Kiswahili for worship as they knew a little and found that some local people knew it. A few more knew Luganda, but they decided to try to learn Lugbara as soon as possible, although they found the tonal nature of the language very confusing. By the end of 1918, they had established three places where Sunday worship took place: Mvara, Ezuku and Eruba. But in early 1919, the influenza pandemic, known as the Spanish 'Flu, reached Uganda. The disease had already killed more people orld-wide than had been killed on all sides in the First World War and it spread rapidly across Central Africa. Both the Gardners and DC Weatherhead became ill. He is said to have told the missionaries: "We could all die and no-one would know." The link to Kampala via the steamers on Lake Albert had broken down as the crews were sick. West Nile was effectively cut off from the outside world. Somehow, word of their plight reached the AIM Congo stations and John Buijse and Mabel Easton came across the border to Mvara to nurse the Gardners. Both Frank and Edith, and their daughter, survived but Edith very nearly died.

Shortly after recovering from influenza, Frank Gardner succumbed again to malaria, which developed into black-water fever. He had already survived four attacks, but now lay close to death. Edith went on praying and eventually, Frank began to recover. But it was clear to them all that he could not continue to live and work in an area where malaria was such a huge threat. Regretfully, the Gardners left West Nile after only eight months, from June 1918 to Feburary 1919. After a very difficult journey, Frank, Edith and Baby Beryl all reached the high altitude AIM centre at Kijabe in Kenya, which was malaria-free. There they both continued to work as missionaries amongst the Kikuyu before they returned to Scotland. They were re-united with their first daughter, Beryl, who was born

in Nyasaland, and had a son, Rex, born in Kenya, to complete their family of three children. Frank Gardner was the man God chose to plant the seed of the Native Anglican Church in West Nile and the man He sustained until the job was done. It was now up to others to water that seed until a rich harvest could be gathered.

Photo of Frank and Edith Gardner and their three children: Rex, young Edith, Mrs Edith Gardner, Frank Gardner and Beryl.

Chapter 4 Watering the Seed
The work of missionaries in the growth of the Anglican Church
by John Haden and David Sharland

If it was the Gardners who had the honour of being the first 'planters' of the Anglican Church in West Nile, who were those who 'watered' this plant and helped it to grow into the Diocese of Madi and West Nile?

The first to follow the Gardners were sent by the **Africa Inland Mission** (AIM). Through AIM, God called members of churches in the United Kingdom, in the United States of America, in South Korea, in Australia and in Canada. These sending churches supported their missionaries with prayer and with funding. Since 1918 over 150 missionaries and mission agencies have played a part in the establishment and nurture of the church in West Nile. From the start, the agreement to ensure that the Church remained Anglican was honoured by all these missionaries, although many came from other Christian churches.

Baptism by immersion at Mvara

In the first five years after the Gardners left Uganda, the next page of the story is about a succession of short-term AIM missionaries who sustained the infant church. Many of them were Americans like the Crowells and the Stilwells. Many were on their way to the Congo. Thanks to them, and to Mr Mount, who came across from Aru in the Congo and was the first to translate Mark's Gospel into Lugbara, the flame of faith was kept alive. But progress was slow. After four years, the missionaries baptised the first group of twenty six believers at Mvara. By 1923 there were missionaries living at Mvara, led by the Rev G B F Morris, who was later to become the first Anglican Bishop of North Africa.

Some came for just a short time, even a year or less. They were volunteers whose friends raised the money for them to travel to and then live and work in West Nile. For some, service in West Nile was their life's work. Some even gave their lives in that service. Ann Morgan came as a teacher to the Arua Teacher Training College, but died of cancer. She was buried in Arua. Douglas and Betty Thornton served at Mvara, but lost their baby son while there. He too was buried at Mvara.

Amongst the many missionaries who came to West Nile, there are those whose long, distinguished service truly 'watered' the growth of the Church. Amongst the AIM recruits, four families and three single women all played a long-term and significant role in the building up of the Church and their contribution is outlined below. All the missionaries and other overseas Christian workers who have served in West Nile are listed in Appendix 1. at the end of the book, with apologies for any omissions. The first of these four families was the Vollors.

**Canon and Mrs Albert Vollor, or 'Bwana Vollor and Madamu Vollor'
– in West Nile 1923-1965**
Albert Vollor might well have died as a child, when tuberculosis nearly took him, but he survived thanks to the God who heard the prayers of his Christian boys' club friends. After study at Cambridge University, he met the tiny Florence, who had left school at twelve to care for her nine brothers and sisters in London's poorest Dockland area. The Vollors were tough, and were attracted to service with AIM because the Mission trusted in God to supply what was needed to do His work. In 1923, they went by sea to Mombasa, by train to Nairobi and on from Kijabe to Kampala, where they met with the Anglican Bishop, and Albert was ordained. Eventually, the Rev and Mrs Vollor reached Pakwach. For the last eighty miles to Arua, they had to walk, with their camp-beds and their meagre belongings on the heads of porters.

It was the Vollors who carried out the pioneering work of establishing the Native Anglican Church in West Nile. Albert became the pastor for the whole of West Nile and was also responsible for schools, but when he arrived, there was no church and there were no schools. There are many stories of their lives in West Nile, of their journeys to visit churches with their young family at a time when lions, leopards, buffalo and elephants made walking, cycling and later driving, very dangerous.

Albert and Florence Vollor, DD

After just two years, there was a proper school at Mvara. Florence soon established a Teacher Training College to provide teachers for the rapidly growing chain of Church primary schools right across the District. In Albert Vollor, God called a man who had faith, organizing ability and a passion for literacy through Primary schools. These were what was needed to establish the Native Anglican Church for as many of the West Nile people as possible, so that the men and women of West Nile could worship God together and their children go to schools where they could learn to read God's word for themselves and so find a faith of their own.

In 1945, twenty two years after they first came to Mvara, Canon A E Vollor wrote a report for AIM setting out the state of the Church of Uganda at that time in the District. His report is a fitting tribute to his own contribution.

> 'The 'Mvara hut' has long since vanished and in its place stands a well-established and extensive Mission Station. At the centre of Mvara Mission, there is the brick-built church called 'Emmanuel', built in 1936 with the help of a gift from Christ Church, Westbourne, through AIM, in memory of the Rev. Trevor Lingley of the AIM UK Home Council. There is accommodation for two thousand people in the church.

The brick-built church called 'Emmanuel'

A little distance away is the school area with classroom and buildings for boarders to care for over one thousand scholars. The rapidly growing medical work has a compound all to itself and is being quickly filled up with medical and surgical units, with all their necessary ward accommodation.

The Bible School is prominent among the departments of work, for here the evangelists, teachers and lay-readers are being trained. The foundations are being laid for the future leaders of the church. The little printing press, groaning for expansion, is working overtime to keep the hungry readers supplied with Christian tracts and evangelical literature.

But Mvara cannot carry the burden alone; this is shared by 109 outposts, scattered far and wide through a parish of 5,500 square miles. We think of this work as a complete whole, inter-related and co-ordinated for area-wide development, with the one aim – the extension of Christ's Kingdom.

The 'little printing press' which Canon Vollor (right) used from 1923 to print many church materials at Mvara.

To undertake this, there is a staff of 194: four ordained men, two European and two African, nine African Lay Readers, 54 trained evangelists-teachers, 70 partly trained church teachers, 53 certificated school teachers, two European church and school workers, one doctor and one nurse……

There are 3,254 baptised church members, 1,150 in preparation for baptism and 5,100 enrolled in the schools.'

This is what 'A'bi', or Grandfather as the Lugbara called him, reported in 1945. The Vollors continued to serve the Church of Uganda for a further twenty years. Before their retirement to England in 1965, Canon Vollor served as Archdeacon of West Nile, and he had the joy of seeing the Rev Silvanus Wani consecrated as the first Assistant Bishop of Northern Uganda – a wonderful reward for all their years of faithful service.

Travel for missionaries in the early days of the church in West Nile

Mr and Mrs Stuart Cole Senior, in West Nile 1926-1940 and Mr and Mrs Stuart Cole Junior, in West Nile 1956-1973

The second family to serve long-term in West Nile were the two generations of Coles. Firstly, the Coles Senior came from Northern Ireland to the Congo with AIM and then moved to support the work at Goli in the south-west of West Nile. An American missionary, Harry Hurlbert, the son of the General Director of AIM, had lived and worked amongst the Alur at Nebbi, near Goli, where he was famous for living in a house in a large tree.

The Alur had responded to the Gospel and by 1923 there were already six churches in the area, each led by an Alur evangelist. Alur Christians had come over from the Congo to preach in West Nile, and the first Alur to be ordained was Apolo Okech, who became Archdeacon and Rural Dean for what later was the Nebbi Diocese. In 1926, a church was built at Goli, in the high country on the Congo border, where Stuart Cole and Albert Vollor had decided would be the best place for the southern centre of the Anglican Church. Soon a girls' school was started and then a Junior Secondary School with Miss Audrey Danby serving as long-standing Head. A dispensary was opened with Barbara Grey as nurse.

Stuart Cole Senior stayed at Goli until 1940, when he and his wife moved to Moyo in the extreme north of the District before going home to Northern Ireland in 1942. It was his son, Stuart Cole Junior, who came with his wife May back to Uganda in 1956. The Coles both came from the Presbyterian Church in Northern Ireland.

Stuart and May were both teachers, and Stuart took over the leadership of Arua Teacher Training College (TTC) from Mrs Vollor, while May taught English. In their seventeen years at the College, they must have trained hundreds of young men and women to be teachers serving in church schools established all over West Nile.

Stuart and May Cole and their three children at Mvara

They also had a strong influence on the leadership of the Church, as it was Stuart Cole who invited the Kenyan Evangelist Joseph Kayo to preach at a mission to the TTC students in 1967. Many TTC students committed their lives to Christ at this Mission. Henry L. Orombi, Isaac Anguyo, John Milton Anguyo, Moses Adraiga, Asnatha Ocokoru, Rhoda Mindreru and many others all made a commitment during the Mission, and others, like John Ondoma, came to the Lord shortly afterwards.

Stuart Cole always encouraged and supported his students to pursue further academic studies after completing their Primary Teacher Training. With Stuart's help, John Ondoma went on to become secondary trained and to take a BA degree at Makerere University, eventually becoming the Headmaster first of Muni Girls School and then of Mvara Senior Secondary School.

The chain of churches and of primary schools had spread right across West Nile, and a start had been made on the Scriptures in the languages of the people of the District. Until 1928, Mark's Gospel was the only New Testament Book available in Lugbara. The Vollors worked hard to produce a translation of the New Testament which was printed by the Bible Society in 1936, but they were not language experts and there were many inaccurate translations. God sent two very different people, both gifted in languages to meet this critical need.

The Rev Canon Seton and Mrs Mary (Peggy) Maclure, in West Nile 1942-1985

Rev Canon Seton and Mrs Peggy Maclure

The Rev Seton Maclure and his wife Mary, known as Peggy, endured a war-time voyage from England in 1942. He was a Cambridge graduate, ordained to the Church of England ministry and sent to Uganda by the UK Home Council of AIM with responsibility for the supervision and training of the evangelists, teachers and lay-readers.

When they first arrived at Mvara, the Maclures worked with the Vollors for ten years to build up the Anglican structures of the church. This meant identifying and training key Ugandan church leaders, many of whom were mentored by Seton Maclure. Their ministry is described in the chapters on African pastors and all would acknowledge a great debt to Canon Seton Maclure.

As a gifted linguist, Seton was keen to learn good Lugbara and Peggy followed his lead. They became well known and loved throughout the District as a couple who would visit village churches to take services and share in a meal of *enyasa*. In the early days, this meant riding bicycles down narrow paths through the high elephant grass to reach villages which had no road access, or using dug-out canoes to cross rivers. Sometimes, it meant being carried by others. Where the Maclures led, other missionaries followed.

In 1959, Seton and Peggy moved from Mvara to Goli to be involved in the work of translating the Bible into Alur. By the time that was finished, the Church leaders in Goli would say that Seton Maclure knew more Alur than the Alur themselves! The Bible Society asked for his help with other projects to translate the Bible into other languages. He chaired the committees which checked the Acholi and Lango translations, and also worked on the Kakwa and Kebu texts in West Nile. In each case, the work depended on the work of a translation committee of dedicated Ugandan Church leaders.

The Maclures brought up their four children at Mvara and Goli and established a centre of hospitality at their Mvara house which became famous throughout Uganda. Many times, Peggy served her 'refugee soup', always available from the vegetables in their garden, which was not only an important source of food but also of seeds, offered with good advice on gardening. Everyone was welcomed - visitors from overseas, missionaries on their way to the Congo and African leaders of the West Nile Church - and there always seemed to be enough for all.

As Seton was responsible for the supervision and training of the Clergy and lay leaders of the Diocese, the Maclures would frequently be away from Mvara arranging for the Bishop to ordain those who had finished their training and were starting their Parish ministry. This involved cramming as many people as possible into their Volkswagen Combi, driving down long earth roads to remote villages and sharing in both the ordination service and an *enyasa* feast with much celebration. There are very many in the Anglican Church of West Nile who remember Seton and Peggy Maclures' kindness and willingness to help individuals and families whenever there was a pressing need.

Peggy Maclure in 1971

Canon Seton Maclure with Bishop Wani at the Ocoko ordination

The Maclure family has continued their support for the Anglican Church in West Nile. Seton and Peggy's daughter, Betty, came with her husband David Payne to visit the Church in 1989. They plan to visit again for the Centenary in 2018.

Mrs Betty Payne, Seton and Peggy Maclures' daughter, at the site of the new Cathedral, when she and her husband, David Payne, visited West Nile in 1989.

Miss Laura Belle Barr, in West Nile 1960-1980
While the Maclures were travelling from the UK to Uganda in the 1940s, the American Home Council of AIM had already agreed that Laura Belle Barr from Philadelphia, USA, should be sent to work in a girls' Primary School in Aru in the Congo, but she did not reach Aru until 1944, two years after the Maclures arrived in Arua.

These two, a British ordained Anglican at Arua and an American member of the Church of the Open Door at Aru, would lead teams of Lugbara church leaders in the task of translating the complete Bible into Lugbara. Their work is a superb example of international and interdenominational co-operation led by the Holy Spirit to meet the key need of the Scriptures in the heart language of the largest group of people in both West Nile and the adjacent areas of the Congo.

Laura Belle first learnt good Lugbara from the senior girls in her school. She had realized that without this she would not be able to serve God in Aru. She would not only learn the spoken language, which at that time had no agreed orthography (rules of written forms and spelling), but worked out how non-Lugbara speakers could best learn it.

Her expertise led to the publication of the first 'Course in Lugbara' in 1961, as the first text book which met all modern academic standards. She explained that the right 'tone' was as important as the right vowels and consonants, as even the shortest words in different tones had very different meanings. This makes learning Lugbara very difficult for Europeans and led the churches in both Uganda and the Congo to set up translation committees.

Laura Belle Barr in 1971

Each month, Seton and Peggy Maclure and Laura Belle Barr met with a translation committee, sometimes in West Nile, sometimes in Congo, often sitting in a village in the shade of a tree. They worked through the Bible, verse by verse, to arrive at a text which was both as close to the original as possible and could be understood by Lugbara speakers. There is a lovely story of their efforts to translate Paul's words in 2 Corinthians 5 v 4, about him 'shedding the earthly tent of his present body in order to get his new resurrection body'.

But there is no Lugbara word for 'tent' and the committee were not happy about using the Kiswahili word '*hema*', as this was used by soldiers with a bad reputation. One of the committee suggested that the idea of a snake sloughing off its old skin was a good way of explaining what Paul had meant. Did not the snake lose its old skin to gain the shiny new skin in all its beauty? Was that not like gaining a 'new resurrection body'? The Lugbara have a word for this 'sloughing off' and the verse had its translation.

Seton and Laura Belle's work was made much easier when she moved from Aru to West Nile in 1960 and made her base at Ringili, near Kuluva. She worked there until the completed Lugbara Bible text was sent to England for checking by the Bible Society. It was finally published in 1966. It was a great day when copies of the new Bible could be bought in Arua and read under the street lights of the town before being taken home to share with the family.

Dr Ted and Mrs Muriel Williams, in West Nile 1941-1979
When Dr Ted Williams and his wife Muriel were sent by the British Home Council of AIM to Mvara in 1941, their ship was attacked by a German U-boat, but the torpedo missed. They knew that the God who had called them to serve in Uganda would not only enable them to arrive safely but also provide for their needs, testing their faith at every stage. Their first 'hospital' at Mvara was a pair of mud-walled thatched buildings with no ceilings. Ted set about turning these into a small medical centre in which Muriel could see the less urgent cases while he also carried out basic surgery on emergencies. An early one was a young man with a strangulated hernia, very close to death. When he not only survived the operation but began to recover strength, Ted's reputation as a doctor with power over witchcraft was assured.

Another early patient was Chief Ajai from the Madi area beside the Nile who had a large growth on the side of his face and several other growths on his body. It took a lot of courage for the Chief to trust the English surgeon, but he did and Chief Ajai not only lost his disfiguring growths but also became one of Ted Williams' strongest supporters. When Ted became an honorary game warden in

West Nile, the game reserve called Ajai was established near to Inde as a sanctuary for the few remaining white rhinos.

But the Williams knew that Mvara was not a good place for a general hospital. It had little land for expansion, was too close to the Government hospital in Arua and was in the middle of a large population of school and TTC students, many of whom came for treatment when not really ill. There was also a pressing need for a centre for the treatment of leprosy, then and now a disease feared by many communities. They found a site about seven miles to the south of Arua which was uninhabited. Two hundred acres by a hill called Kuluva was leased for the use of the hospital and an access road put in. A further 1,000 acres was leased for leprosy patients to live in eighteen villages, each serving patients from one of the District's counties. This enabled Ted Williams to try a new leprosy drug which could be dispensed regularly to patients without them having to travel, an approach which proved very effective.

With the workload growing at Kuluva there was a pressing need for another full-time doctor. Ted's brother, **Dr Peter Williams, with his wife Elsie** joined the Kuluva team in 1950. Peter began an eye clinic at Kuluva which helped many to improve or regain their sight.

The Williams family with Granny Williams in 1971

Not long after, their parents moved from Kenya to help with the practical tasks of building and maintaining a large hospital with very little money but a lot of faith. Their father, **J.H. Williams**, was an engineer who oversaw the building of cottages for the families of leprosy patients, and the main buildings of Kuluva Hospital.

The Williams started a training scheme for trusted members of staff to become nursing aids, dressers and evangelists, as the preaching of the Gospel was always part of the medical and surgical work of Kuluva Hospital. Alongside the two doctors a succession of nursing staff came from AIM UK to serve at Kuluva, starting with Margaret Miller in 1953, then Pat Whisson and Edith Samuels from Australia in 1954.

Though the 1950s and 1960s, AIM UK sent many nurses to serve at the hospital, perhaps the longest serving in Uganda being **Maureen Moore,** who joined Kuluva in 1966 but moved to Kagando Hospital in 1986 and continued to serve there until retiring to the UK. Another long serving AIM missionary is **Dr Keith Waddell,** who joined Kuluva in 1964, retrained as an eye specialist and is still working at the Ruharo Eye Hospital at Mbarara.

When at the time of Amin's Coup, Uganda lost about half of its trained medical staff, responsibility for Kuluva Hospital was handed over to Ugandan leadership. Shortly afterwards, Ted Williams fell and broke his hip, but Archbishop Wani managed to persuade the military to allow MAF to evacuate Ted to hospital. He did return to continue his work at Kuluva, and he and Muriel retired back to England in 1979. They left a centre of medical and surgical excellence that had by then established a fine reputation across Uganda and well beyond. There is an account in a later Chapter of this book which tells the story of how God used the start that was made at Kuluva to grow into a health care service for the whole of the district.

Through AIM, God called families: the Vollors, the Coles, the Maclures and the Williams to serve His Church in West Nile. He also called many single people, with three single ladies playing especially key roles in the growth of His Church. Laura Belle Barr was one and another was Margaret Lloyd, who arrived in West Nile not long after Laura Belle.

Miss Margaret Lloyd, in West Nile 1946-1979
Margaret was sent by the British AIM Home Council to serve as a teacher at the Arua TTC at Mvara in 1946, at a time when the Anglican Church in West Nile was developing Primary education throughout the District but had no secondary school. The CMS, the Catholics and the Colonial Government had all founded secondary schools in other parts of Uganda, but developing secondary education was less important to the Vollors than training Primary teachers at Arua TTC.

Margaret started her teaching in Uganda at Arua TTC, but as a secondary trained biology and RE teacher she was asked, with Mr Gillman, to develop a Junior Secondary School in 1949. The 'pioneers' of Mvara JSS, as the members of the first secondary class were called, included Bishop Remelia Ringitho, with Margaret Lloyd as Head. The school flourished, and many of the future leaders of the Church were educated at Mvara JSS before going on to complete their secondary years at other schools such as Sir Samuel Baker Senior at Gulu.

Towards the end of Margaret's service in West Nile, Archbishop Silvanus Wani invited her to write an account of her work. Her book 'Wedge of Light' became an account of the Revival Movement in the Diocese. She wrote, that she enjoyed her teaching at Mvara but was conscious that others had more joy in their service of God. Then one day, as she was praying, she wrote: 'Suddenly Jesus met with me. I had a great consciousness of the Precious Blood of Jesus washing my heart and my burdens rolled way. Then came a deep sense of peace…'

Margaret Lloyd

Margaret became very close to the Brethren who had

been touched by Revival, especially Rev Silvanus Wani, Rev Benoni Obetia, and Rev Silas Androa.

When in 1959, the decision was made to open a Senior Secondary School at Mvara and to close Mvara JSS, Margaret was appointed as the first Head. She served until the mid-1960s when Lewis Stephenson took over the leadership. They were both involved in the huge expansion of Mvara SSS through the late 1960s and early 1970s when a two form school grew to four forms of entry and then further developed to S5 and S6. A new campus was built as part of a World Bank funded programme on what was called 'The New Site', nearer to the town of Arua.

Throughout this period, Margaret remained the fiercest defender of the Church status of the Mvara SSS, with a Board of Governors chaired by the Bishop. Sunday services were compulsory for all the students each week. She championed the place of Religious Education on the timetable and her oversight of the girls who were boarding at Jerico in Mvara where the girls' dormitories were located, was both firm and very effective. But with the rapid expansion of the school, the move to the New Site and the need for more and more teaching staff from a very wide variety of backgrounds, Margaret's influence in the school was reduced. She continued to teach at Mvara SSS until she retired in 1976.

In 1979, she was able to revisit West Nile to join her friends in the Revival Movement for a convention and to complete the last two chapters of her book. "The only institution," she wrote, "to come out stronger from the fire (of the Amin years), was the Church…as the Church of God grew." Her prayer at that time was that "this growth might continue until Jesus comes again."

Miss Joy Grindey, in West Nile 1962-1996
To the Lugbara, the third of the single ladies was 'Gurindia', but her English name was Joy Grindey. After growing up in England and studying at university, she worked for a time before hearing a call to missionary work and was sent by the British Home Council of AIM to serve initially at Mvara in 1962. Joy was a

gifted linguist and worked at first with Seton Maclure on Bible translation before moving to a small hut in a village outside Koboko to start the translation of the Kakwa Bible. Rev John Dronyi, a Kakwas, joined Joy on this translation project until the task was completed and the Kakwa Bible published in 1983. She also worked on the text of the 'Kebu Bible and became an expert on the languages of West Nile.

Quiet, unassuming but always smiling and laughing, her Kakwa nick-name of 'Ajonye' or 'laughter' was the finest compliment that they could pay to one who devoted her life to give them God's word in their heart language.

Joy Grindey (left) and visitor at her Koboko house

Joy returned to England in the 1990s and lived quietly in retirement in Beccles, Suffolk. To keep remembering Uganda and the people Joy loved, she called her house in England "Namirembe", which means House of Peace. In 1999, Joy died peacefully in Suffolk, and was cremated. She had requested that her ashes be brought to West Nile. They were laid near Koboko, in the land she loved so dearly. Huge crowds gathered to witness the final resting of one they so loved and respected.

Other Christian Missions and Christian workers
Up to Independence in 1962, many of those who worked in Uganda's schools and colleges were serving as missionaries. In the case of West Nile, at Mvara Senior Secondary and at Arua TTC, many of these had come through AIM. After 1962, when the Government of Uganda insisted that all teachers in Ugandan

schools and colleges were employed as Government Education Officers, those teachers who had come with AIM transferred to Government Service and new recruits came through the British Overseas Development Agency.

However, many had a Christian commitment and these retained their Mission or Church links. Later, after the time of Idi Amin and the second Obote regime, other Christian Missions became involved with the Diocese of Madi West Nile. Mission Partners serving with Church Mission Society (CMS), with the Leprosy Mission and other Christian Missions came to help.

John and Ihla Hooyer, at Mvara 1984-1990.
John and Ihla Hooyer came to West Nile from the U.S.A. where John was City Administrator for Boulder City, in Colorado. John used to say, "Our life in Boulder was just too comfortable. We both felt God's call to live life more on the edge." They applied for mission service with Christian Reformed World Relief Committee (CRWRC) and were accepted, thus beginning a long-standing partnership between CRWRC and the Diocese of Ma'di and West Nile.

In 1984 John and Ihla finally arrived in West Nile, where life was much more 'on the edge' than it is today. Damaged buildings, very rough roads, half empty shops and few vehicles were seen in Arua. John and Ihla lived up to their motto so often quoted by them, from Joshua chapter 1: "Be strong and courageous". Their life in West Nile was also marked by kindness and compassion.

John was the first CRWRC Partner to Madi and West Nile Diocese and worked with the Christian Rural Service (CRS) at Mvara, Ringili and within the Parishes of West Nile. It was their aim "to serve people whose life was difficult." In West Nile they found the reality of that calling. CRWRC later became World Renew, as it is known today.

In West Nile, John found many challenges, but also much fulfilment and deep friendships. He was a popular worker for Jesus and His Kingdom. He always exuded a message of hope and healing after the difficult years of unrest and war.

John encouraged hard work, but it was always flavoured with joy. In CRS, he was a great team worker and team builder, travelling many rough miles to encourage farmers and CRS staff. At first, John was seen as a 'father figure', then more as a brother as the CRS team got to know and trust him more deeply. He had a great sense of humour – often ragging his colleagues and raising the mood of the day.

John and Ihla worked well with Bishop Remelia, and he recalls several occasions when John willingly helped him out, when he had problems with his vehicle. Gadi Bileti was his friend and co-worker within CRS, and his death from a bullet in an ambush at Mount Wati in Terego, came as a deep, deep shock to John. Gadi was on his way back to Arua from Moyo, on CRS work.

John was keen and ready to learn from his colleagues, and maintained a strong personal discipline; he was keen to cooperate for the greater good. He was always sensitive to the local culture, but keen to promote appropriate change, where he saw lives could be improved.

A verse often in his thoughts and influencing his actions was Joshua 1 v.6
'Be strong and courageous, because you will lead these people to inherit the land I swore to their forefathers to give them. Be strong and very courageous."
This happened to be the verse he had planned to use the day after he died. It was a guiding principle to his life. Sometimes he had to stand up strong, as his faith led him to challenge some attitudes in those he worked among, but John always sought to avoid conflict, wherever possible.

Sadly, John died in a car accident on the way to Kampala, where he was travelling together with Ihla, Sister Margaret and a driver, in the CRS Land Rover. He was buried in Mvara, a symbol of his love for the place and people. It was during his burial that news arrived of Bishop Ephraim's death in Kampala. What tragedy hit West Nile, but even such calamity could not dampen the fervour of God's faithful people, and CRS went on from strength to strength.

A Conference facility was built at Ringili to remember John and further his vision of training farmers to live a better, more informed life, with Jesus at the very centre. After his death, the CRS work continued, but ended during the difficult times the Diocese went through. Now, the agricultural extension and rural community development work in the Diocese continues in the demonstration farm at Mvara with support from CMS.

The German Missionary Medical Team (GMMT), in West Nile 1982-2006

GMMT was started by two German Doctors, Werner and Irmela Wigger. They began working in Kuluva Hospital in 1982. They established a Nutrition Unit in the Hospital in the form of a ward for malnourished and other chronically ill children, with a teaching room for the parents. GMMT sent a total of fifteen German Missionaries to serve at Kuluva and in West Nile whose names are listed in the Appendix. They served even at very difficult times at the hospital and among them was **Birgit Klumpp** who served as a nurse and as a health worker at Kei Health Centre in Aringa. Birgit has wriiten an account of her experiences in West Nile between 1986 and 2006:

Birgit Klumpp's West Nile Story
Kuluva Hospital: September 1986 – August 1987, April – July 1989; Kei Health Centre, Aringa: January 2001 – August 2006
"It all started in 1986 when I left my little home town near Karlsruhe in Germany for a one-year-assignment at Kuluva Hospital with the German Missionary Medical Team. I'll never ever forget our welcome in West Nile: actually nobody expected us when we got there. We were the first Germans who made it in one day from Germany to Arua!

The first weeks we spent in a thatched hut with killer ants as regular visitors. It took some time to get adjusted to the stable-like patient rooms, to all the poverty, to losing pediatric patients due to lack of oxygen or lack of essential drugs. I got used to the terms "out of stock", or "the man with the key is gone" or "come back tomorrow".

I was also confronted with robbery and killing when we were for a short assignment at Goli. Why did God spare my life, but Jackson, a father of four kids, got killed? That experience left a deep impact in my life. During the remaining months at Kuluva I often went with the Primary Health Care (PHC) team to the villages and worked at "Centre Block" (the "Kuluva-ICU") together with Sister Irene and Sister Edith. It was a time that definitely left its mark on me.

During that time, Isaac & Sally Anguyo became dear friends. Isaac already had his dream of starting a ministry among the Aringa. Once he even took a team of us on a trip to Aringa – it was a district still suffering from year-long rebel activities. People were just returning from exile, being forced to start their lives from scratch. Shortly after that trip 'Here is Life' was founded and one of the many visions was to start a medical work in Aringa.

It took several years, many sincere prayers for guidance and clarity, another four month assignment at Kuluva Hospital, and a trip in 1998, and a two year "detour" to a refugee camp in the Philippines to prepare me for my years in Aringa. In the meantime the security situation in Aringa had improved and "Kindernothilfe" was able to build a health centre at Kei. It was the right time to start a medical project among the people in Aringa. It was clear to me that God had prepared me all these years for this new challenge and so I accepted when Christian Services International (CSI) asked me if I would be willing to work at Kei Health Center (KHC).

In February 2001, I returned to Uganda as "Kei Health Center Primary Health Care Coordinator". When Isaac took me on my first trip to Kei, it was another unforgettable experience: a two-hour-ride from Arua on bumpy, rocky roads – or should I call them paths? Kei seemed to be the end of the world with people sitting idle under the mango tree at the trading centre being curious about the first Muzungu who was supposed to live and work with them.

Isaac Rembe soon became not only my best co-worker and translator; he also patiently taught me the Aringa language and culture and became a very good friend. Together we would ride our bikes to visit the Kei people in their homes, trying to win their trust and introduce Health Care to the communities. It was also the time when HIV prevalence was at the highest in Uganda, one of the two leading countries in the world in the fight against HIV/AIDS. This might have been true in all the other districts in the country, but Aringa had been neglected and left out in that fight. But we not only set up a well functioning immunization program, we also put emphasis on HIV/AIDS sensitisation and prevention.

Birgit Klumpp and Isaac Rembe

The first responses in the communities were quite skeptical, but later on people were willing to join the fight of HIV/AIDS. In cooperation with the AIDS Information Centre we became one of the few HIV/AIDS testing centers in Aringa. We founded the Post Testing Club (PTC) and with support from "Help for the Brethren" we were able to build a PTC Center at Kei Health Center, which included a well-stocked library and a generator-operated TV set.

Rembe and I made countless trips to Tuliki and trained several villagers in Community Based Health Care, so that these village health workers could teach people in their village what they were taught. It was amazing to see how things in that Muslim community changed, and it was a joy and blessing for us to see how we could help people grow.

Everything just seemed to go well; we were thankful for the many different programmes we had been able to start at Kei and other communities – and then things just changed, literally in an instant. In March 2004, an American missionary couple and a student got killed at the Evangelical School of Technology in Aringa (ESTA), and nobody knew what the motive for that cruel attack was. My life also changed overnight, when soldiers were sent to protect the Kei Health Centre (KHC) compound. I had to live with snoring soldiers on my porches, who were supposed to be protecting the only Muzungu at Kei. It was a very difficult time, not knowing if the ESTA killers had also planned to attack Kei. But I knew that God still wanted me to continue with our projects and not to leave my friends, colleagues and the villagers alone.

But a year later, things got even worse. More than 400 prisoners escaped from Arua Prison, among them the suspects of the ESTA killings. HIL and the local police could no longer guarantee my safety, so I suddenly found myself a refugee at Kuluva Hospital and later in Arua in the house of missionaries on leave. Twice a week I was allowed to visit Kei riding in a police car with heavily armed policemen, not being allowed to move around freely and not allowed to go for outreaches to the communities, something I had really enjoyed very much for years.

I had trained my co-worker Rembe for a long time to take over responsibility for the PHC department with all its activities and so he officially took over my job as Kei-PHC-Coordinator. After a big farewell party in Kei with hundreds of people attending, with sadness and yet with peace in my heart I left my "Kei-family" and the place that was my home for five and a half years and returned to Germany in August 2006."

Alastair and Sheila Taylor - at Ringili 1990 – 1995
The next missionaries to work with the Madi and West Nile Diocese were the Taylors. Alastair Taylor was born in Bristol, in the UK in January, 1963. After graduating, he married Sheila, who was from the Isle of Wight, in the south of England.

Alastair and Sheila arrived in Arua in January 1990 to work with Christian Rural Service (CRS) and were based at Ringili Theological College. The Taylors had a passion to use their agricultural skills to demonstrate the love of Christ by helping people to do better at their farming so that they would be able to feed their families, buy the essentials they needed for home life and also have enough money to support their local church.

The Taylors were seconded to the Diocese by Tearfund UK for just four years, but they extended this to six. Alastair's local counterparts were Abindu Nelson and Isaac Yikii. During their time at Ringili they had their children, Nathaniel and Leonie.

The Ringili Tree Nursery.

Together they established "Ringili Demonstration Farm" where Alastair and Abindu taught the theological students agriculture and then set up an agricultural outreach programme to support farmers throughout the Diocese, which at that time also included what is now Nebbi Diocese. As the team developed, David Acidri Onzima joined them, as the accountant.

The demonstration farm became a very popular training venue, with community groups coming from across the Diocese to spend time learning about the different farming and income generating options at the farm. Communities always had to contribute something towards their training and as money was in short supply, this was often in the form of cassava flour and beans, with chickens, which the training centre cooks transformed into tasty meals. This was important, because a key assessment of any training for the participants was if they were able to gain weight over the three or four days of training, as assessed on the Taylors' weighing scales!

Transport was in short supply in West Nile in the early 1990's. Tear Fund provided a Mitsubishi pick-up to support the work of Ringili Demonstration Farm, and this took staff out to the contact communities and also brought community members to Ringili for training. On one such journey, they were stopped by the traffic police. The community members got out of, and off the pick-up. When they were counted by the police, the number came to 32….. However, the police were happy with the work that Ringili was doing and told them to load the car back up and proceed…carefully!

Comfort and Nathaniel at the training vehicle

On one occasion a "bee-expert" came from Kampala and wanted some honey comb to use in a training which he was doing. It is usual to do bee work at night, but he said he could handle the bees in the daytime.

Suddenly, there was a banging at the door and it was the bee-expert chased by swarming bees seeking refuge! Apparently the West Nile bees were not that keen on being disturbed during the day. The expert was badly stung and the Ringili Principal - the Rev Enyabo – and the Ringili bee team had to rescue the situation through donning bee suits and wet towels to put the lid back on the hive.

Alistair and Sheila hosted many visitors from other parts of Uganda, Zaire, as it was then, and overseas. It was while house-sitting for the Taylors that I (David Sharland) met my wife, Heather, who was attending a Community Health Conference at Ringili, organised by Tear Fund. The family cat was caught in a trap in the woods. I cleaned the wound, but it needed stitching. I went in search of a courageous nurse, and found Heather!

Ringili also became the training ground for Tear Fund interns. Alistair Seaman, Angus Murrey and Simon Darling were those who spent a year living in a grass roofed house in the Taylors' garden, and worked hard with the programme. Each of them made a special contribution to the life of Ringili.

Nathaniel Taylor, Moses Opifeni (on bikes) and friends by Ringili Guest House.

The Ringili Demonstration Farm training centre and the hostel building were made possible due to a generous donation from Ihla Hooyer, the wife of John Hooyer, who was tragically killed in a road accident close to Nebbi, about 6 months after the Taylors arrived in Ringili.

Alastair and Sheila left Ringili to return to Britain for the sake of their children's education, for Alastair's further studies and to take up a post as leader of the Kulika Trust work in Berkshire. They later returned to Uganda for work based in and around Kampala.

Allan and Anne Lacey - in West Nile 2007 – 2013 .

Allan Lacey was born and grew up in London. Rural West Nile was a very different environment for him. Anne grew up in another great city, Liverpool. After marriage, Allan was ordained in the Church of England, and Anne worked as a Nurse Teacher and researcher. They made their home in South Yorkshire, where they parented Ben and Joanna. It was after taking early retirement from Parish life that Allan and Anne offered for Mission Service with the Church Missionary Society (CMS)

When they first came to West Nile, it was to Kuluva that they came, living in one of the staff houses on the hill. After a short period at Ringili, Allan began to work with pastors and church teachers more widely within the diocese. Anne, who was a well qualilified Nurse Tutor with a PhD in Public Health, offered her skills and passion to the health work of the Diocese. She also helped develop and implement the training for the Diploma in Nursing course now offered at Kuluva.

After three years, they returned from leave to settle nearer Mvara. Allan saw a greater need to encourage pastoral care for the under-resourced pastors in the parishes. He started the Parish Ministries Department at the Diocese Headquarters, and travelled extensively to experience the realities of pastoring in remote rural Parishes. Seeing a great need for materials to encourage their ministry, Allan developed the 'Lectionary Link' materials, first in English and then in major local languages. This first came out as a monthly publication and was then compiled into a three volume set to cover the three liturgical years. This initiative was to encourage informed, Biblical preaching throughout the Diocese. It is still a valued resource today.

Also, springing from his passion to see the strengthening of the Parishes through Biblical teaching and discipling, Allan developed a link with the Langham partnership. They joined him in running annual training weeks with Preachers' Clubs and Refresher Courses for pastors to keep the flame alive! This too has proved a long-lasting relationship that continues. The need to print written training materials led Allan to start the Reprographics unit in Mvara. This has become a thriving business, but also gives a vital service of printing and photocopying within the Diocese.

Anne was instrumental in revitalizing the Health Department of the Diocese, and opened the Health Office in the Secretariat at Mvara. Not only was Kuluva Hospital overseen from this office, but the six Health Centres of the Diocese as well as community outreach, were administered from here. Cindy Okullo was recruited to join the Diocese, from Lira, and has ably succeeded Anne in this post, and has carried it forward to an even higher level.

Allan and Anne feel thankful to God and greatly privileged to have had the opportunity of sharing seven years of their lives with their brothers and sisters in West Nile, and count it as one of the richest experiences of their lives. Some of their favourite memories from that time include arriving in remote parts of the diocese after a long and dusty drive to be welcomed with exuberant singing and dancing; learning (after much impatience) that life can be lived to the full without reliable electricity, water and all the things that westerners depend upon so much; seeing individuals grow in faith and maturity, and handing over key elements of ministry to local Christians, who were well able to continue after we returned home; discovering the joy and unconditional faith in God's provision of our fellow Christians who often experienced considerable hardship; exchanging knowledge of each other's culture – including learning to love enyasa(!); the beauty of Uganda, with its wonderful scenery, plants and animals.

Allan and Anne returned to the UK in 2013 to their much loved and missed family, and to enjoy their second retirement! They remember that Ugandan smiles are the best in the world and say: 'To God be all the glory for all He has done!'

Chapter 5: The Growth of the Church in West Nile

5.1: Population, Infrastructure and Ministry by the Rev. Canon Isaac Candia

"The message was preached in ever widening circles. The number of believers greatly increased...." Acts 6:7

I. Growth in Ministry

By the early 1940s, Africa Inland Mission had laid a strong foundation for the growth of the Church in West Nile under the able leadership of Albert Vollor. With a well-established Mission Station at Mvara, a rapidly growing education system and medical work, and a prominent Bible School in place, there was a substantial local team of people to grow the ministry of the Church. Schools and Churches were established across the region, most of which growth was now demand driven. As the new believers scattered into the various corners of West Nile, their lifestyle and testimony spread like wild fire. Key cultural and opinion leaders came to Mvara to request for Churches to be established within their villages. They donated chunks of land free of charge, for the Church to occupy under a 'Temporary Occupation Lease' and these were recognized by the government. With all this the Church now entered the phase of consolidation.

In 1940, Vollor was the only priest in the region. On 5th March 1943, Silvanus Wani and John Dronyi were ordained and more parishes were opened. Silvanus Wani was sent to head a new parish in Koboko, while John Dronyi remained in Arua. Later other people joined the ordained ministry. Benoni Obetia was sent to open a parish in Vurra and Appolo Okech was stationed in Goli. From these parishes, more and more parishes came into existence so that by the end of the 1940s, the West Nile Archdeaconry within the Upper Nile Diocese which had its headquarters in Buwalasi, Mbale, had the largest number of parishes.

When the Madi and West Nile Diocese was created out of the Northern Uganda Diocese in 1969, Goli, Arua and Koboko Archdeaconries were created.

With the ever increasing number of Churches and parishes, it was inevitable that more Archdeaconries be created. In 1974, Madi Moyo and Oyibu Archdeaconries were created, then Maracha Archdeaconry in 1976, Vurra and Terego Archdeaconry in 1988, Rhino Camp Archdeaconry in 1992, Aringa Archdeaconry in 1994, Arua Urban and Emmanuel Cathedral, in 2008 and finally, Logiri Archdeaconry in 2018. In 1993, Nebbi Diocese was created out of Ma'diand West Nile Diocese.

The progress of the gospel is often largely shown by numerical growth. By the time of the Celebration of the Centenary of the Anglican Church in West Nile, there are 12 Archdeaconries, 138 parishes and 627 Churches. The population of members of the Anglican faith has grown to about 556,300. The Bishop confirms about 15,000 Christians annually.

II. Growth in infrastructure.

Rev Albert Vollor was not only involved in organizing the Church, he was also a practical leader, who was involved in developing infrastructure – especially in the construction of Churches and Schools. Many of his workers called him 'aguaka', which means 'bed bug', because when he planned to do work, he kept a close watch over it and stuck to it. He would surprise his workers at any time, catching them unawares. He encouraged every community where evangelists were sent, to construct churches, once the land was commissioned by him as a Temporary Occupation License (TOL). Most of the congregations honoured him by inviting him to identify the right site for the Church and bless it. His measuring tape was his feet strides, and people would often enjoy seeing him mark off the site for the church construction.

Most churches were grass thatched with walls made of mud and wattle, but a few were semi-permanent, with brick walls 14 inches thick and grass thatched roofs. Vollor had some specially trained people who went around doing the roofing for the Churches and Schools. These included Apollo Oruma, Yoana Ewaa, Dison Palaa, Enosi Alonzi and others.

Africa Inland Mission taught the Christians not to depend on external support for developing their Churches, but to raise their own resources locally. While Emmanuel Cathedral was considered the best Church in the region, Christians began to plan to build another Cathedral to the glory of God. In the late 1940s, a Committee was set-up to plan for the new Cathedral. Each Christian was tasked to pay a fee towards the project. It, however, took a long time to do the ground-breaking for the new Cathedral, because in the 1960s, most churches began to plan to improve their own churches to take care of the ever increasing number of Christians. To some, the money for the new Cathedral was being misappropriated. They preferred focusing on developing their own Churches.

However, the Cathedral Committee continued to get collections through Baptism and Confirmation fees and in the mid-1970s, they bought a Tata lorry that would later help in transporting materials for the project. Unfortunately, during the Liberation War, the lorry was robbed and all was lost.

Bishop Wani was more concerned with the task of organising a new Diocese than building a new Cathedral. Bishop Remelia Ringtho's times were tough and difficult when Idi Amin was in power, and there was scarcity of almost all necessary items needed for development. Then came the Liberation War. It was when Bishop Ephraim Adrale came into office in 1988 that he resurrected the Emmanuel Cathedral Building Project. He did not live long enough to see the foundation dug, but he had laid the foundation stone in 1991.

The project was eventually followed through by his successors: Bishop Caleb Ariaka Mawa Nguma, Bishop Enock Lee Drati and Bishop Joel Obetia. Some of the people who contributed to the completion if the new Cathedral were Mr. George Okai, Mr. Odama Richard and Mr. Edison Adiribo, who served as Project Committee Chairmen; and Rev. Can. Matia Matayo Anguandia and Rev. Gadi Angundru, who served as project clerks.

On 2nd December 2007, the old Cathedral was decommissioned and released to be used for other purposes. The new one was consecrated by Archbishop Henry

Luke Orombi. In 2017, the Diocese, with support from CMS Ireland, renovated the old Cathedral to be used by the Cathedral as the Children's Church and by the Diocesan Youth Department as a centre for youth training and discipleship programs. While the New Cathedral now stands to testify to the ability of the local church to be self-supporting and self-sustaining, the newly renovated Old Cathedral stands to testify to our desire to preserve our history and our commitment to children and youth ministry. These, we believe, are the church today and the church for the future. As the Lord said, "Upon this rock, I will build my Church." May the Old Cathedral live to produce the seeds for the growth of the Church in West Nile.

As the Cathedral got organised, down in the Parishes and Archdeaconries, the Christians continued to have fundraising events to improve their Churches. All initiatives were spontaneous and self-driven by the laity. From the 1960s a number of Church buildings were transformed from temporary to semi-permanent and later still to permanent structures. The following table shows the current level of growth in infrastructure (from unpublished work by Can Elly Nayenda).

Table showing status of church buildings

	Archdeaconry	Permanent	Brick/Grass	Mud/Grass	Under Trees
1	Emmanuel Cathedral	1			
2	Aringa	14		12	3
3	Arua	72		4	
4	Arua Urban	8	4		
5	Koboko	28	6	6	2
6	Maracha	61		1	2
7	Oyibu	20		14	14
8	Rhino Camp	18		35	6
9	Terego	52	2	4	3
10	Vurra	59	11	5	1
	TOTAL	**333**	**23**	**81**	**31**

While there seems to be rapid development in the construction of churches, staff housing remains a huge challenge. Most clergy and lay readers live in 2 to 3 roomed houses of mud and wattle with grass thatched roofs.

Map of West Nile showing the Archdeaconries of the Madi and West Nile Diocese and Nebbi Diocese in the Centenary Year 2018 by Kumbuka Ronald

5.2: The Work of African Evangelists in Planting Anglican Churches within West Nile by Rev Can Alfred Jeth Adiburu

The words of our Lord Jesus Christ, recorded by St. Luke in Acts 1: 8 b "… and you will be my witnesses in Jerusalem and in all Judea and Samaria, and to the ends of the earth." (NIV) came true in West Nile Region in 1918, when Africa Inland Missionaries, Mr. Frank Gardner, his wife, his three month old daughter and his brother Alfred Gardner arrived to start evangelism in the region. After these pioneers came, other missionaries followed, whose activities are also covered in this book.

It was not only the work of the missionaries, from Europe, USA and Canada that helped in evangelism in the region, but African evangelists also played a vital role in evangelizing the region. Therefore, my emphasis will be on their role in planting the Anglican churches within West Nile.

When the missionaries came, they embarked on teaching the Africans reading, writing and some arithmetic. In order to make this teaching effective, the missionaries started a Preparatory School at Mvara. It was from this School that the African Evangelists were first produced. Some of the learners from the School became teachers, and started to teach other Africans, while others became church teachers and were used for evangelism and planting churches in different parts of West Nile.

The work of the African Evangelists was very effective. Many people knew how to read and write because of the efforts of these African Evangelists. The condition set for baptism was that one must learn how to read the Scriptures before being baptised. So this made people put a lot of effort into learning to read. The African Evangelists did not only put emphasis on church planting and teaching the catechism, but also established village schools within the church premises. The writer of this article is one of the beneficiaries of a village school started by an African Church teacher.

The Church in West Nile Region has grown large in number. In Madi and West Nile Diocese alone, there are now 627 churches. If we are to take Nebbi Diocese also, we can then say that there can be close to 1000 churches in West Nile Region now. Each of these churches has an African Church teacher or Evangelist. At the moment, it will not be possible to write something about each church Teacher, but I will try to limit myself to a few examples of the African Evanglists, especially the early ones.

The first church started by the missionaries was at Ezuku. Mr. Tomasi Awutumbe, from Ma'di Okollo, was the first church teacher. After Ezuku the missionaries started the second Church at Eruba. This was their resting place from Ovisoni on their way to Mvara, where they were given a place to establish a mission station. Tomasi Awutumbe also worked as church teacher at Eruba (now called St. Paul's Church, Ewava). While working in Eruba, in 1926, Tomas Awutumbe started a church at Ambala, on Okojova Hill.

In 1927, Israel Avijo, from Anzu in Vurra, replaced Tomasi Awutumbe as a church teacher for Eruba. He also worked at a church at Ambala and established another church at Okuvu (the present Kuluva Parish).

Stanley Ozimati from Congo worked as a church teacher at Natete in Kampala. He was teaching the catechism in a hidden place for fear of the Kabaka (King) of Buganda, because of deaths of the Christian Martyrs which he had ordered. The major martyrdom took place on 23rd June 1886, where 23 Anglicans and 22 Roman Catholics were burnt or clubbed to death. From Natete, Stanley Ozimati came to work as the Church teacher at Eruba. He was ordained at Mvara, and became the first Priest of Eruba Parish.

Benoni Obetia was from Ezuku, and first worked as a school teacher, but later became an Evangelist until he was ordained. He was the Rural Dean for Vurra and Ma'di. The day he made a pastoral visit to Ma'di Okollo was the very day Bishop Joel Samson Obetia was born. That was why the retired bishop was named Obetia.

The Rev Benoni Obetia was the first person who organized fundraising for building the new Emmanuel Cathedral at Mvara. But unfortunately the new Emmanuel Cathedral was built when he had gone to rest with the Lord, so he did not witness the consecration of the new Cathedral in 2007.

Rev Benoni Obetia

One of the great African Evangelists was Kezekia Ajule from Omi in Ajara, Ayivu County. After his primary four, he went to Makerere College and trained as a teacher. He was a great footballer, and played for West Nile Region. Rev Albert Vollor, the first Archdeacon for West Nile Region, sent Kezekia Ajule to work as church teacher at Nyiovura, in Adumi Sub-county, Ayivu County. After Nyiovura, he was transferred to Moyo. Kezekia Ajule got an opportunity for theological training in the Sudan.

After the training he came back to Mvara, and was training those who would be ordained clergy or who would be sent to work as church teachers. Kezekia also worked in Anyavu in Vurra. He got an opportunity of going to study in United Kingdom. He worked as Assistant Archdeacon, and when Rev Albert E. Vollor left in 1963, Rev. Kezekia Ajule replaced Vollor as the second Archdeacon for West Nile Region. He has passed on and is now resting with the Lord.

Ven. Kezekiah Ajule

One of the African Evangelists, whom the people he worked with will not forget, is Amos Otulua. He is believed to have been born in 1917 in Terego County, Arua District. He was recruited into the King's African Rifle and fought in the Second World War. After the war he returned home in 1946 and got married to Sarah, and God blessed them with 14 children: 8 boys and 6 girls. Amos was admitted to "First Letter" training as a Church Teacher in 1955. After completing his training he was posted to Nyiovura Church. In 1957 he returned for "Second Letter." He was sent back to Nyiovura. After the "Third Letter" he went back to Nyiovura. Amos did many wonderful things. Many people converted to Christianity and were baptised. He had skills in masonry and carpentry. He used these skills to build a better church at Nyiovura. He also planted a good number of acres of eucalyptus trees for the church.

In 1960 he became an Area Leader and was transferred to Urugbo. He only served here for one year. The Christians in Mvara requested for him and he was posted to Mvara. He worked in Mvara for five years and later was posted to Ociba Church of Uganda on the eastern side of Arua Town. He planted a large garden of eucalyptus trees for the church. When he retired from Ociba and died on September 9, 1999, he was buried in a grave he had prepared for himself and his wife at their house in Mvara Sudan Zone.

South of West Nile Region is the area occupied by the Alur. There were also some great African Evangelists who evangelized in the area. The south of West Nile became a separate Archdeaconry called Goli Archdeaconry (the present Nebbi Diocese, formed in 1993 by the division of Madi and West Nile Diocese). Examples of African evangelists who worked in Goli Archdeaconry were: Zephaniah Uramba, who spent his youth in Atiyak and moved to Goli. He was the father of Chrispo Uzele, who did great evangelism in Kuluva, and was the head of the Trumpeters. Both Uramba and the son Uzele have passed on and are now resting with the Lord. Other African Evangelists from Alur land who could be remembered were Abram Ndeyeka from Nyapea, Nathanael Onong from Paidha, who was later ordained, Temeteo Uruthwum from Okemu in Warr, Saul Okwong, the father of Rev Can. Ephraim Odoktho, also from Warr.

Some of the African Evangelists in West Nile Region came as a result of the Revival Movement that moved across East Africa. In March 1939 the Revival Movement reached Arua through Dr. Lubulwa. The Revival changed the lives of many people in the region, including those who were already working in the church. The Revival Movement's great African Evangelists were: David Asendu, Sila Drakua, Tefolo Debo, Phinehas Gipatho, Samuel Tholu'ba, Michael Onale, Barnabas Avinyia, Samson Avua and Yoramu Sarua.

Dr. Joe Church, William Nayenda, Yosiya Kinuka and Dr. Lubuluwa were working together as a team in the Revival Movement. Time came when Dr. Joe Church had to go to England on leave. He took William and Yosiya with him for evangelism in England. Since Dr. Lubulwa was not chosen, and was desperate to go to England, he decided to break away and lead his own revival. He made himself a megaphone out of an old paraffin tin and through this he would blast out congregations as they issued forth from their churches. When Dr. Lubulwa reached Moyo, his preaching touched Sosthenes Ajuku who was by then teaching in Primary school. Ajuku gave his life to Jesus Christ, and began to follow Dr. Lubulwa. In 1949, Sosthenes Ajuku started this Movement in West Nile. Some of the people who are still in the Movement are Yoram Sarua (who heads the movement in West Nile region) and others. Now they prefer to be called Chosen Evangelical Revival (CER)

African Evangelists, through the Revival Movement, have done a great work which has changed the lives of many people. Through them many people have come to accept Jesus Christ as their personal Saviour and Lord.

May God continue to work through the African Evangelists to bring more people to the Lord in the next 100 years.

5.3: The Growth of the African Ordained Ministry by Canon Isaac Jaffer Anguyo

The Gardners from AIM were the ones who planted the Seed of the Gospel. The early missionaries continued to water the seeds which germinated, and the African clergy joined them in the watering and harvesting of the work which was started in 1918. It is the aim of this chapter to especially document who the African clergy have been, and who continue to water and harvest what was planted by the Gardners. Only a few of these clergy can be mentioned here. Names of clergy ordained from 1943 to 1968 are listed in Appendix II.

Venerable John Nahumi Dronyi
The first two African priests to be ordained in West Nile in 1943 were Silvanus Wani, who became the first Bishop of Ma'di and West Nile, and John Dronyi, who became the Archdeacon of Koboko. Venerable Dronyi was born in about 1912 to Abe of Godria clan of Kakwa and Gonya of Ndriba clan of Kakwa.

He got married to Ludia Apita from Nyangilia Clan in Koboko and God blessed them with ten children: three boys and seven girls, about fifty seven grandchildren and over one hundred great grandchildren. Venerable Dronyi educated all his children. One became an engineer and his daughters mainly took up teaching. One of the grandchildren, David Dronyi, is a medical doctor.

John came to Arua looking for a job. He was employed by Rev Vollor as a house boy and Vollor saw the potential in Dronyi. He asked him to join the school at Mvara in 1931, where he studied up to Primary Four, then joined the Elementary school and trained as a teacher, teaching for a while.

Venerable Dronyi and Bishop Silvano Wani together joined Buwalasi College from 1940 to 1942 for theological training. Both were ordained in 1943. John came to work in Mvara, Moyo and Koboko. When West Nile Archdeaconry was divided into three Archdeaconries, he worked as the Archdeacon of Koboko Archdeaconry. This covered Moyo, Aringa, Koboko and Maracha.

While at Koboko, John Dronyi encouraged Joy Grindey to move from Mvara and to live in a house in a village near Koboko. He worked together with Joy to translate the Bible, Prayer and Hymn book into Kakwa, assisted by a translation committee. The Bible was completed and published in 1983.

His daughters remember their father mainly riding his bicycle in his work. This meant covering the distance from Maracha to Adjumani and reporting to Arua from Koboko. According to Janet, all this riding affected his health. Dronyi served in this position as an Archdeacon until he died on November 7, 1980 and was buried at Mvara at the Old Emmanuel Cathedral burial grounds. His wife Ludia died in August 2004 and was buried next to her husband Dronyi.

He died during the time where there was insecurity all over the area. Many went into exile. Dronyi was sick at his home in Mvara but his children could not leave him to die alone. They chose to look after him. Dronyi's daily prayer was, "Father, my God, keep my children who have chosen to look after me safe. Let none die." Indeed God answered his prayer. There were deaths around Dronyi's home but none of his children died during the war.

The daughters remember how they lived in the father's house. Their house had open doors, visitors to their home were always welcomed and there was always enough food to feed extra mouths. Dronyi helped to educate many, including needy children from Congo and Sudan. They continue to remember him in these countries for his kindness.

Ven Canon Sila Tileku Adroa by Adiribo Edison
Sila Tileku Adroa was born in 1911 in Paranga Parish, Maracha District in West Nile, to Tileku and Deborah Adee. He spent his early years in Paranga until his father died and the family moved to his grandmother's home at Retriko. The name Adroa literally translates as "from uncles" in Lugbara.

He went to school up to Primary six and then Junior three, when he was identified by the Church Teacher in Paranga and sent to Mvara for Lay Reader's training. After finishing the "First Letter" he was sent as a Church Teacher

(Olupi) to Yivu in Maracha, Wandi in Terego and Aroi in Ayivu. He returned for "Second Letter", after which he was posted to Nyangilia in Koboko.

In 1953, he was sent for Pastors' Training in Buwalasi Theological College, where he graduated as a Deacon in 1955. He was then ordained as a full Priest in 1956 and sent back to West Nile, where he was posted to Adjumani to start the Parish which saw the establishment of faith in the Ma'di community. He then moved to Nyoro in Maracha to start a new parish, which became Maracha Archdeaconry in 1976, where he served up to the time of his death. While in Nyoro he was given the opportunity to undergo Training in Theology in Great Britain for three years.

He was very close to his fellow Archdeacons, Ven Canon John Dronyi of Koboko, Ven Canon Benon Obetia of Vurra and Ven Canon Hezekia Ajule of Arua. He was well known to Bishop Henry Luke Orombi, who frequently refers to Silas when he is preaching. Having served under four bishops, Ven Adroa is said to have been the one who convinced Bishop Enock Drati to leave USA to come and lead the troubled flock of Ma'di and West Nile Diocese, after the deaths of the bishops Adrale and Ariaka.

Silas Adroa was married to Yemima Adroa from Kimiru in the current Oluffe Sub County, Maracha District in the early 1930s. The couple was blessed with four male and four female children. Unfortunately, Yemima was called to the Lord in 1975 after battling with diabetes for over ten years. This left Adroa a widower for one year before he remarried to Tabita Ticia Adroa in 1976. They were blessed with two boys before he died.

Ven Silas Adroa was very keen on education and he educated all his children who rose to national and global prominence. His daughter, Kay Amin Adroa, went to Mvara SS, Gayaza High and Makerere University. She worked for Radio Uganda. She was married to Idi Amin Dada, the President of Uganda. Unfortunately, she met her death in a mysterious circumstance in 1973. Her death was a great temptation to the faith of Ven Adroa, but with the strong belief and trust he had in his Lord, he was able to stand firm and endure this tragedy with the Lord on his side.

His son, Wilson Jurua Adroa, graduated from Makerere University and had a Masters from Canada. He was employed in the Parliament in 1960s, and was later the Permanent Secretary in Ministry of Tourism in the Amin Government. Sadly, the day he learnt of the death of his sister was the day he went to exile in 1973, where he later died in 1984 in Great Britain.

The other children namely John Adroa, Jimmy Adroa, Christine Adroa, Charles Isua and Samson Adroa have all died, leaving only two of his biological children, namely Penina Adroa who got married in Nairobi, Kenya, and Akole Adroa. But the Lord has blessed him with over twenty grandchildren and many more great grandchildren.

The late Silas Adroa will be remembered for the establishment of most of the churches that stand in Maracha Archdeaconry. These Churches attribute their calling to the influence of the Ven Adroa, whom the Lord used to encourage them. He supported many needy children financially to acquire education. His home was always full of children whom he supported with education. He was very keen on farming as such his home in Nyoro was surrounded with granaries which will be filled with food reserves for years. None of the land around his homes in Paranga and Nyoro was idle.

Ven Adroa will be remembered for being approachable, kind and loving. He was resourceful, enterprising and above all committed to his calling to serve the Lord he loved even at very difficult and trying times in his life. He ran a good race and contributed to the spreading of the Gospel throughout West Nile.

Can. Elija Anguli'bo
One of the clergy who contributed very much towards the development of the Church, especially in Madi Okollo, is Canon Elija Anguli'bo. He was born to Aluma and Pirisila Orikoa of Terego Oninia, in about 1918 around the time the

missionaries brought the Gospel. Angulibo got married to Ludia in 1944 and they had seven children. At the time of writing this book six have died and only one is alive.

Not much is known about his formal education. The record available on him is service as a clergy in the Church. He was ordained in 1951 and served briefly in his own county. From 1953 he was transferred to serve in Jiako in Arua Archdeaconry and 1954 was transferred to work in Madi Okolo and later inducted as archdeacon when Madi Okolo was made into an Archdeaconry. He served in this position until he retired in 1997.

The Madi remember him for good work. He encouraged people through his pastoral visits. He won many people to Christ. He also encouraged local leadership. From his work two bishops came from Madi: Bishop Caleb Ariaka and Bishop Joel Obetia. At the time of his retirement, the Christians gave him a gift of two cows. He lived a peaceful life after his retirement until July 6, 2008 when he went to be with his Lord.

Canon Aarona Agoro Dravu

Agoro Banya Aarona Dravu was born on 17th February 1916 to Banda Idroru and Araba Omuru at Mingoro. He was married to Euodia Angolita, daughter of Mukii Dina Ajio of Komogo Mikiti. God blessed Aarona Dravu and Euodia with eight children. At the time of writing this book, two of the children have passed on to live with the Lord. Despite the meagre wages of the clergy, the Dravus educated their children well. All of them are in high positions. One of their granddaughters, Everline Anite, is a Minister in the NRM Government.

The Dravus loved other people; they looked after children not necessarily related to them and according to those who knew them, the doors of their home were always open to anyone who needed help.

Mr. Dravu went in 1930 to an African Inland Mission (AIM) village primary school in Mvara, where he studied up to Primary 4. In 1935 he dropped out of school and travelled to Kampala to seek employment. He was employed by some Indians as a House Keeper and a salesman in their shop. He made very many friends and learnt very many languages. He kept his faith and was baptised on 11th Nov. 1937 by Rev Canon Anania Binaisa at Namirembe Cathedral and was confirmed the same year on 22nd November 1937 by Bishop Stuart at Namirembe Cathedral.

In 1938 Aaron Dravu returned to Arua and settled at Okaiva on Western side of Arua Town. He worshipped at the Native Anglican Church (NAC) in Pajulu Church. He felt called to serve God and in 1945 started his church work as a Catechist at Pajulu Church.

He attended a theological course called First Letter at Mvara. Thereafter he served as Catechist and Lay Reader in a number of churches, he progressed with his studies of Second Letter, and, in 1953, Third Letter. He then went for one year's teacher training at Arua Teachers Training College in 1955. In 1956 he was sent to Buwalasi Theological College and continued with his theological studies up to 1958.

On 8th February 1959 Dravu was ordained Deacon by Bishop Russell, at Ezuku Church in Vurra. After ordination he was posted to Logiri Parish and worked as a Deacon under Rev. Hezekiah Ajule's guidance. On 20 December 1960, he was ordained priest and was posted to Aringa to open the Aringa Parish, which covers the whole of Aringa County. At the time of writing this book, there are now eight parishes in Aringa.

While in Aringa, he made friends with both Christians and Muslims. In this way he was able to sow the seeds of love, unity, Christianity and salvation without fear among the Muslims. The seed he sowed was watered by those who came after him. This made many Muslims, including Canon Isaac Jaffer Anguyo, to convert to Christianity. He was not in a hurry nor used force to convert people to Christ, but was patient with the Aringa.

On 28th February 1963, Rev. Aaron Dravu was transferred to Anyavu as Parish Priest of Logiri. While there he planted eight churches. He also helped to unite the Revival groups in the area who were hostile to each other before he came.

He achieved and changed many things in the churches under him. He preached love, unity, forgiveness, purity and hard work. His house was open to many. He mentored some of his Christians to priesthood. These include: Late Rev Canon Sosthenes Enyabo, Late Bishop Ephraim Adrale, Rev Peter Ogani, Late Bishop Caleb Ariaka, Rev Kiliopa Nyati and Rev Musa Drandua. He encouraged Bishop Remelia Ringtho in his development into the ordained ministry.

Dravu continued with studies. In 1969 while he was serving at Logiri Parish, he went for a 6 month Post Ordination Course at Bishop Tucker Theological College in Mukono and in 1974 he went for Urban Church Training Course in Trinity College Nairobi for three months.

Dravu left Logiri parish in 1979 and during the Liberation War, he briefly went into exile in Congo. He returned the same year and settled at Awindiri until the end of the instability.

In 8th Feb 1980 Rev Aaron Dravu was transferred to Akua Church of Uganda in Terego County to establish Katrini Parish. He served God with all his might and built a big house for the Parish priest. He sowed the seeds of salvation, love, unity and forgiveness in the parish and all churches under him. He served God in Akua Parish for eleven years. He had a break of two years when he established his home at Mvara Sudan Zone.

When there was a need for a Parish Priest at Ociba Parish in Arua Urban, on 8th Febraury 1993, he was called to fill the place and served here for two years He retired due to poor health, diabetes and hypertensionand went to live with His

Father in Heaven on 26th November 2005. He was buried in the Old Emmanuel Cathedral Cemetery by the retired Rt. Rev. Dr. Joel Obetia.

This is what the children say about Dravu's wife, "Euodia, was far-sighted, a mother to all, a mentor and a counsellor. She encouraged Dravu to press on when faced with challenges in his service."

She was bed-ridden for 15 years and he took care of her patiently, with love and affection till death parted them. She followed her beloved husband on 1st July 2009 to live with their Father in heaven.

Rev. Canon Semi Draku

Canon Draku was baptised in May 1954, and confirmed in July 1956. He got married to Rachel in a traditional ceremony on 1962 and wedded in 1965. He was ordained as Deacon on 1977, was priested in 1979 and made Canon on 1985. He was inducted as Archdeacon in 1988. He was the first Archdeacon of Terego Archdeaconry. Draku has vast work experience. He taught in Are Primary School in 1960 – 1962. This school was established by the late Odayo Kamure. Draku worked as Adult Literacy Supervisor for Terego County under Culture and Community Development from 1963 – 1964. He joined church ministry as church teacher at Church of Uganda, Paranga in Terego County in 1964 – 1966. He then worked as an Area Leader of Church of Uganda Aiivu area from 1967 and was then appointed as a typist/ secretary in the Bishop's office of Madi and West Nile Diocese in 1970 – 1973. In 1977 Draku served as Deacon/typist in Mvara Parish and Diocesan office.

When he was ordained as a Priest, he was posted to Mvara Parish from 1978 – 1987. After being inducted as Archdeacon, he then served in Terego Archdeaconry from 1988 – 2006. While working as the Archdeacon, he also worked as the Bishop's Commissary in the Diocesan Office from 1992 – 2005.

During the time he was in the Bishop's office, he would ride from Terego, work, and return to Terego. He did these roles concurrently with the Archdeaconry work.

Draku retired from active work on 31st December 2006. The Lord blessed Canon Semi and Rasili Draku with ten children: two girls and eight boys. Despite the meagre wages of the clergy, they managed to educate all their children. All of them are employed. From the family has come the seventh Bishop of Madi and West Nile Diocese, Rt. Rev. Charles Collins Andaku. The family has established Wandi Progressive Secondary School, and indeed it is a progressive school.

Canon Timoteo Enima.

Canon Timoteo Enima was born around 1918 in Terego County in Arua District to Ndaa and Dede. Both parents were from Terego. Enima got married to Holda Ondretiru in 1938. They were blessed with nine children; six boys and three girls. At the time of writing this book, they are survived by one son and three daughters. Their remaining son, Gideon Nyakudri, before retiring served in a number of schools as teacher and headmaster. One of Enima's daughters is Canon Salome Candiru Anguyo. She served as a teacher and a tutor until she retired and is now serving in the Arua District Service Commission. In the church, she has served as the President of Mothers Union and a member of the Cathedral Council.

Enima has grandchildren who are serving at both district and national levels. Three of them should be mentioned: Alfred Cox Anguzu serves in the Public Service, his brother Ronald Ocatre has served in the Health Ministry in many capacities. In 2018 he is studying medicine to become a medical doctor.

Engineer Aita Joel has won engineering projects in the country and outside like Malawi.

Enima went for Primary school education in Mvara. He did not go far with formal education. He joined church work as a warden at his home church in Drikpara, and worked as Church teacher and Area Leader in the following places: Jiako in Arua, Paranga in Maracha, Nyori in Aringa, Obongi in Madi, Baito in Madi Okollo and as an Area Leader at Bongova and a Tutor at Ringili Rural Trade School.

He was ordained as a deacon in 1963 and went to work in Adjumani until 1966, when he was posted to start Oluko Parish in Arua Archdeaconry. In 1974 he was made a Canon and posted to work in Wandi Parish in Terego Archdeaconry. At the time he started working in Wandi Parish, Terego was still under Arua Archdeaconry. He was the one who initiated the process of making Terego an Archdeaconry.

Enima was one of the early church workers whom, you feel, had received the call to serve the Lord. Much of his early life was in very difficult places. Many termed going to Aringa, Moyo, Obongi and Adjumani as punishment. But he went willingly and served the Lord with love.

He was exemplary in marrying off his daughters at very low bride prices. The clan people did not like him for this, but he stood his ground. Their home had open doors to children who wanted to live with them and go to school. The home was also open to many Christians in the Parish. This was true when they worked in Oluko. The priests who came to work after him found it hard to fit in the place.

Enima retired in 1987 and died in 1988. His wife Holda died in 2017, and both of them are buried in the Drikpara Church compound.

Rev. Erinayo Kule

Rev. Erinayo Kule was born in April 1924 to Erema Agotre and Sarah Odu in Oleba Sub County in Maracha District. He got married to Edith Nola Maaru in 1949. God blessed them with eight children. Three of the children died including the only boy in the family. The children were highly educated. One of the girls, Joyce Drijaru-Yikiru, committed her life to serving with Life Ministry (Campus Crusade).

Kule went to Nyangilia Primary School, then to Buwalasi Teacher Training College in Mbale. He served as a class teacher for a short time and became a headmaster of Arua Demonstration School. While there, he also served as the Madi and West Nile Diocesan Minute Secretary/Treasurer. He was ordained as a deacon in 1972 and priested in 1973. He continued to work as headmaster and priest (Tent-maker) in Emmanuel Cathedral. He passed on while in service.

Kule combined civil work with Church work very well. He advocated for well-being of clergy, upheld work ethics. Teachers liked him, and he helped many of his teachers with their personal problems.

Some people who knew Kule well had these things to say: "An educationist, giving equal opportunity for both boys and girls, he enabled the poor to study", "He was a good administrator, promoted a conducive environment for service especially for the teachers." "He was highly disciplined and ensured discipline, industrious and a man of high integrity." "He was orderly and loved cleanliness and took cleanliness as his life-style. He modelled what he believed." "Kule is known to have worked with minimal complaints."

5.4: The Work of Missionaries from West Nile in the Karamoja Diocese of the Church of Uganda by Rev Christopher Yikii Agatre

The clergy and lay people of Madi and West Nile Diocese were inspired by the Great Commission in Matthew 28:18-20, to take the Gospel to other parts of Uganda. In Karamoja, North East Uganda, something unique happened when the Karimojong warriors killed their first pastor called Akamu Zephania in 1952 for preaching the Gospel. The second Karimojong pastor was Rev Rufusi Lorukude, who escaped death from warriors narrowly on many occasions.

The killing of the first Karimojong pastor inspired believers from Madi and West Nile Diocese to go as missionaries to Karamoja in the 1960s and 1970s supported by the Diocese. Nine believers went for missionary work to Karamoja. They were: Nathaniel Abiku (1962), Rev Can Manoa Ofuta (1963), Ezekiel Obiayi (1962), Yovan Draa (1970), and Ramu Agatre Okitta (1971). Others came from Nebbi Archdeaconry which was then part of Madi and West Nile Diocese. They were: Ephraim Nyingwa (1969); Hilkia Obia (1971); Joram Okoku (1971) and Kiliopa Ochaya (1970).

Some of these people have gone to be with the Lord. We thank God for ably using them as Missionaries to Karamoja. The Diocese sent willing Christians to Karamoja as indigenous missionaries. The purpose of this part of the chapter is to tell their story and experiences and the impact they had on the Karamojong and the Diocesan Christians.

According to Rev Can Manoa Ofuta, Christian missionaries go in obedience to God's call. Jesus assured us that missionaries will face persecution and suffering. Missionaries leave friends behind, experience culture shock and rejection (Matthew 10:16-31). But instead of falling into self-pity or pride, they learn to delight in serving God. Rather than being a burden, obeying His call brings joy and reward in heaven. Therefore, a missionary serves not out of duty but love (2 Corinthians 5: 14-21). Rather than seeking personal gain while witnessing,

Christian missionaries bring glory to God by honouring Christ's righteous life, sacrificial death, and absolute authority.

A Karamojong village poses for a photo

A missionary addresses his congregation in Karamoja

Karamoja, Uganda

Rev. Can. Manoa Ofuta further revealed that the youth got saved in Karamoja and as a result, one of the leading youths became a Bishop in Karamoja in 1980. He was called Bishop Peter Lomongin and he (Rev Can Manoa Ofuta) was the Bishop's Commissary. The youths who became pastors as a result of mission work in Karamoja were: Rev Niconora Lopul, Rev Isaac Longole, Rev Peter Logit and Rev Odunge Samuel.

However, in 1977 President Idi Amin, who was against whites as a result of his anti-western foreign policy, sent away Bishop Brian Herd, who was then the Bishop of Karamoja Diocese. During the same period Rev Limlim John and a District Education Officer called Andrew Adupa were killed for preaching the Gospel. The missionaries built a Church at Namalu, the Archdeacon's house at Nabilatuk (Pian County) and the Pastor's house in Kaabong.

The missionary work of **Ramu Agatre Okitta in Karamoja** was obtained from his diary, documentaries and testimonies by his children. He was born in 1930 to Late Barnaba Okitta and Late Odraru Okitta of Embario (Odule'ba) Clan, in Ocoko, Ajia sub-county, Vurra County, Arua District. **Rhoda Ofutaru Agatre** was born in 1938 to Late Timeteo Odulua and Late Erina Odulua of Abira Clan, in Ocoko, Ajia sub-county, Vurra County, Arua District.

They served as missionaries for nine years in Karamoja region. Amongst their achievements were the planting of churches in Karamoja where there were no churches before. These were: Karenga Church, Lobalangit Church, Loyoro Church, Kidepo National Park Chaplaincy (Church of Uganda), Karpedo, Church and others. Some of the Churches they planted grew larger to become Parish Headquarters. For example, there is now: Karenga Parish, Loyoro Parish, and Lobalangit Parish.

They trained and mentored Karimojong youths, some of whom have become pastors and Archdeacons in North Karamoja and Karamoja Dioceses. For example, Ven Can Lopeyok John, who is an Archdeacon in Kaabong Archdeaconry in North Karamoja Diocese.

During the night of the 1976 Christmas Day, over twenty Karimojong warriors attacked the Agatre home. Their reason for the attack was to pick the Christmas offertory which these warriors had seen Christians give in the Church earlier. Ramu Agatre neither succumbed nor relented to the demands of the Karimojong warriors, inspite of their breaking two windows of the house to forcefully get the Church's Christmas money.

In the end, God was the family's victory. Ramu Agatre overpowered one of the Karimojong warriors by capturing the spear from the warrior's hand through the broken window. This was miraculous in that all the warriors had to flee in disarray. In Karamoja, when you disarm a warrior of his weapon, he flees. God was at work in His protection of the Family (Psalm 121: 1-8).

Upon returning to West Nile in 1979, Ramu Agatre delivered the spear, which he had captured from the Karimojong warrior, to the Bishop's Office at Madi and West Nile Diocesan Secretariat, Mvara. We learnt that the Army took away the spear from the Diocesan Offices (Bishop's Office) when they broke into the Offices during the 1980-1981 war that had engulfed the whole West Nile region.

God also saved Ramu Agatre on preaching expeditions during the nine years of serving God among the Karimojong (1981-1979), from the attack of a lion, from flooding rivers and from warriors, all during the time they were there. What an opportunity they had to preach the gospel where few missionaries have preached.

Rev. Canon Captain Manoa Ofuta

Canon Manoa Ofuta was born in 1939, Ayivu County, Arua District to Teleo and Amule Ondurua. He remembers that both were not Christians, but later his mother was baptised Penina. Unfortunately, his father never became a Christian and Manoa never saw him die because the father died while Manoa went to work in Karamoja. Ofuta got married to Holdah Ajidiru on 27th December 1962 at Church of Uganda Jiako. They were blessed with six children. By the time of writing of this book, one of the children had died.

Ofuta started his primary education in 1952 in Cilio Primary School in Terego. After four years in Primary, he joined Mvara Rural Trade School (RTS) in 1956. He learned carpentry.

In his own words: "When I received Jesus Christ as my Lord and personal Saviour, I was completely changed. I joined RTS then later joined B.A.T and worked for six months. I lived in Sudan zone, Mvara, and I had my own workshop, where I made a lot of furniture and sold them.

In the year 1962, my brother Nathaniel Ejaa offered to go to Karamoja as a missionary. In 1963, Nathaniel invited me to Karamoja as an agricultural instructor. The first thing I was asked to do on arrival, was to build a house with local materials. The following year Rev. Cutright was asked to send students for lessons in agriculture, but none came."

Then in 1964, Ofuta became a church teacher, without any training. He said he did the work of the church hand in hand with building houses in the Archdeaconry Headquarters. The white missionaries loved what Ofuta was doing, preaching the word of God and building houses. He was sent to Church Army Training College, Nairobi from 1968-1969. This was the beginning of his preparation for full ministry for the Lord.

In 1970, Ofuta was commissioned Church Army Captain. He started to work with Bishop Brian Herd and an African missionary from Soroti called Yovani Mukula. He was appointed the Diocesan Treasurer and Secretary in 1971. In the same year he got funds from the German Bread For The World Mission to build a Community Centre in Moroto. Ofuta was ordained Deacon in 1975 by the Rt. Rev. Silvanus Wani and ordained priest by Rt. Rev. Brian Herd at St.Philips Church in Moroto while he was serving in Karamoja.

In 1977, when Archbishop Janani Luwum was killed, shortly afterwards, Bishop Brian Herd of Karamoja was deported. Bishop Herd entrusted the running of the diocese to Ofuta. Some Karamojong pastors wanted Ofuta to be the next Bishop, but he refused saying, like John the Baptist, he was only a fore runner and could not take possession of the diocese. As the in-charge of the diocese, he transferred one of the pastors, Peter Lomongin, from Nabilatok to Moroto town. Later he was appointed the Bishop of Karamoja. That is how Rt. Rev. Peter Lomongin became the first Karamojong bishop.

In March 1979, the Ofuta family returned to West Nile. Rt. Rev. Remilia Ringtho asked Ofuta to head Muni Parish which was curved out of Oluko Parish. While at Muni Parish, Ofuta was appointed the chairman of the mission department. Just as Ofuta was settling in Muni Parish, the Liberation War broke out. The remnants of Amin's Army waged war with the Liberators. When the remnants retreated they left the civilians at the mercy of the Liberators.

On one fateful day, as gunfire rocked the district, Ofuta looked towards Ocoko, southern side of Arua Town, and saw a lot of smoke rising from houses being burnt. He went back to the church and told the people there to flee and save their lives. Many left; his family went to his village home in Terego. Ofuta went to Congo. But some of his friends at Muni Primary School thought that it would be safe. That same day, eight of his friends: Michael Borua an MP, Gayo Chaka and two of his children, Samuel Atonya, Yuda Bileti, the Area Leader, Isaac, and Okello were killed and left to rot.

Ofuta stayed in DRC for three months. He came back to Muni to find no houses. While he continued to work at Muni, he was appointed the Diocesan Treasurer in 1982. The following year he was appointed the Diocesan Secretary. On 24th December 1985 he was transferred to the diocesan offices and given a post as the Estates Officer. He renovated the houses in the Diocesan Headquarters.

During the 1986 war Ofuta did not go anywhere. In his words, he wanted to prevent people from taking advantage of the war and looting diocesan property. He decided to hide such property as type writers and record books in a sewage tank. He drove the motor vehicle and motorcycle to Oliri Parish Ezoo in Zombo

District, while a carton of hoes was taken to Yole. After hiding this diocesan property, he informed Bishop Henry Luke Orombi, as a witness, so that if Ofuta died in the war, Bishop Orombi would recover them. After the war he brought back all the items he had hidden.

Ofuta continued to work as the Diocesan Treasurer, Secretary, Mission coordinator and Estates Manager. He helped to build a house for Mothers Union worker. During this period Ofuta also worked with Kuluva Hospital rebuilding project from 1983-1995. He also worked with Ambassadors of Hope from 1987-2015. Through this project many orphans have been helped to get education and giving them hope in life.

When in 1990, Bishop Adrale passed on at Nsambya Hospital Kampala. Ofuta remembers how devastating the news was. Just as he had been when he was in Karamoja, Ofuta again became the chief administrator in the diocesan office. Rt. Rev. Silvanos Wani who had retired was asked to work as a caretaker Bishop for Madi and West Nile diocese for one year, until in 1991 Caleb Ariaka Nguma was consecrated and enthroned bishop of Madi and West Nile diocese. Ofuta was appointed bishop's chaplain and still held his other responsibilities. After two years Bishop Caleb died in a motor accident and Bishop Henry Luke Orombi became a Care Taker Bishop of the diocese.

In 1994 Enock Lee Drati was consecrated and enthroned Bishop and Ofuta continued as his chaplain. The other responsibilities were given to other people. On 24 December 1999, Ofuta was posted as Vicar of St. Philips Church, Arua and worked here until end of 2005. Joel Obetia was consecrated the Bishop of Madi and West Nile Diocese in 2005, he asked Ofuta to serve him as his chaplain in 2006.

Ofuta retired in 2007 at the age of 65 but continued with the work he started in 2001 as a visiting Chaplain at Arua Referral Hospital and Arua Government Prison. After retirement, he became full chaplain in the two institutions. In 2014 he handed over Arua Government Prison's chaplaincy to Captain Nelson Nguma.

By the time of writing this book, Ofuta is still the Chaplain of the Hospital. One project in his heart is the Church of Uganda Chapel at the Hospital. He has completed building the walls.

After conversion and joining the East African Revival, Ofuta made a complete commitment for his Lord, in whatever place and whatever condition and time, he will go and do the work willingly. At the age of 77, Ofuta has the energy to lead worship, preach, and visit the sick and comfort at funerals. He is one person the present generation will need to learn from.

Chapter 6: The Bishops of the Anglican Church in West Nile by the Publicity Committee of the Consecration of Bishop Collins Charles Andaku, and Moses Aluonzi Alaka

The First Bishop of Madi and West Nile Diocese: Bishop Silvanus Wani 1969-1977

Bishop Wani was born in July, 1916 in Adakada village in Nyangilia, Koboko District, the son of Kakwa parents, Mana Ada Wani of Nyangilia Clan and Miriam Ddaa, of Drimu clan. His early education was at a bush school at Nyangilia, Koboko and then at the Primary School at Mvara. He was baptized on July 9th, 1931 at Nyangilia Church and confirmed on September 20th 1935 at Emmanuel Church at Mvara. Silvanus decided to train as a Primary teacher and then attended up-grading training for teachers at Kampala Normal School attaining a 'Grade A' Teacher's Certificate. He was chosen to go to an AIM church teacher training establishment at Adibu in the Congo and began his teaching career at Mvara Elementary Primary School. In 1938, he became a tutor preparing students for the Grade 'C' teachers' qualification at Mvara.

Silvanus married Penina Yopa of Kupera clan in Lobule sub-county on June 20th 1936 at Emmanuel Church, Mvara. She was a vernacular teacher and served the Lord with Silvanus faithfully until her sudden death in Kampala on 25th May 1982. Because of the War in Luwero and insecurity in West Nile, she was buried at Namirembe Cathedral. The Wanis had ten children, eight boys and two girls.

<u>Bishop Silvanus Wani and His wife Penina</u>

God called Silvanus to the full-time Ministry and he and John Dronyi joined the ordination course at Buwalasi Theological College. They were ordained as deacons in March 1943, then priests on 5th March 1944, the first Ugandan deacons and priests in the West Nile District.

Silvanus was sent to serve as a Curate in a new parish in Wandi in Terego, but he was drafted in 1944 into the King's African Rifles, becoming a part-time army chaplain. He served in Kenya, Somaliland, Ethiopia and Burma until the Second World War ended in 1946. Silvanus returned home to become a parish priest at Mvara, where he stayed until 1950. While at Mvara, and always keen to improve his own education, he used correspondence courses to pass O levels in English, Mathematics and Geography, with the help of Canon Seton Maclure and Miss Margaret Lloyd.

In 1951, Silvanus became the parish priest in charge of Koboko, Yumbe, Maracha, Moyo and Adjumani, all now districts of West Nile Region. He spent a year in the UK at Oakhill Theological College for an Advanced Certificate in Theology from 1955-56, before returning to Koboko for three more years.

In 1960, Silvanus moved to Gulu to serve as the Diocesan Secretary/Treasurer of the Diocese of Northern Uganda, under Bishop Keith Russell. While in this post, he spent a year studying 'Christianity and Islam' at St. George's College, Jerusalem. On returning to Uganda in June 1964, Silvanus became Assistant Bishop of the Diocese of Northern Uganda consecrated in Namirembe Cathedral by Archbishop Leslie Brown. Wani went on to become the first Ugandan to serve as Bishop of Northern Uganda, and from 1964 became Chaplain General for Protestants of the Uganda Armed Forces, serving in this role until 1978.

In 1969, when Bishop Janani Luwum took over as the Bishop of Northern Uganda, Silvanus became the first Bishop of Madi and West Nile Diocese. In 1974, as the most senior bishop, he was elected to be Dean of the Province of the Church of Uganda, Rwanda, Burundi &Boga-Zaire and served in this role until

March 1977. In that year, Archbishop Janani Luwum was killed and Bishop Silvanus Wani was elected Archbishop. He also oversaw the maturing of the church in Rwanda, Burundi and Boga-Zaire as a new Province.

In retirement after January 1984, Silvanus Wani led a quiet pastoral life, helping out in various churches in Madi-West Nile in support of the Diocesan Bishop, until his death in 1998. He had served as a bishop for twenty well-spent years, as the pioneer Ugandan bishop of both the Diocese of Northern Uganda and of Madi & West Nile. He was the incumbent Archbishop during the Church of Uganda Centenary celebrations, laying the foundation stone for Church House to mark the Centenary.

He steered the Church of Uganda through its most difficult period during the military regime of Idi Amin, with the killings of his predecessor Janani Luwum together with two Government ministers, and the persecution of other Christian and political leaders.

As Archbishop and Bishop of Kampala Diocese, he helped establish new churches, especially in the depressed areas of Kampala, including the Okuvu (Lugbara) Church.

Throughout his time as Priest, Bishop and Archbishop, Silvanus Wani travelled all over the world on behalf of the Church of Uganda. He attended the 1968 and 1978 Lambeth Conferences while Archbishop, and was invited to attend the exclusive Haggai Institute for global "proven, credentialed leaders" from the developing world.

Bishop Wani accepted Jesus Christ as his Lord and Saviour. He became a member of the East African Revival. He did not like the clerical titles and preferred to be called, "Adripi Silivano" meaning Brother Silvanus. He helped the members of the East African Revival to focus on Scriptures.

The Second Bishop of Madi West Nile Diocese: Bishop Remelia Ringtho 1977-1988

Bishop Remelia was born on October 21, 1929 at Warr in Okor Zombo District. His father was the Okor King, Okuendru Pandaleo of Alur, and his mother Oriemu came from the Kebu tribe. He married Eunice in August 1953 and they were blessed with nine children, five boys and four girls. Remelia first went to school at Mvara in 1942, for P1-3 and then to Goli for P4-6, before joining the Junior Secondary School at Mvara as one of the ten pioneers taught by Mr Gilman and Miss Margret Lloyd in 1949.

On leaving school, he went back home to teach at Okemu in Warr for two years, before returning again to Mvara for the first Lay Readers course in English. He then worked as a teacher and Warden in Goli Junior Secondary School. He was converted in 1949, and decided that one day he would leave teaching and become a pastor, because he loved the Lord. In 1960 he joined the Ordination Course at Buwalasi and obtained the Provincial Certificate before being ordained by Bishop Russell at Awindiri Church in 1963.

Bishop Remelia had this to say, "I was posted as a deacon at St. Philips Church in Arua in the same year. St. Philips then was a white church, all the wardens were Europeans, and we started to build St. Philips Church together until 1965, when I went to Britain for a two year Diploma in Theology course. After two more years back at St. Philips, when the Madi and West Nile Diocese was created in 1969, I became the first Diocesan Secretary and Treasurer until 1974, when I went to Bishop Tucker Theological College as its bursar for two years.

"After a year back in Arua as Assistant Bishop of Madi and West Nile Diocese, I was consecrated and enthroned as the 2nd diocesan Bishop by Archbishop Wani on September 4, 1977, and worked as the Diocesan Bishop until I retired in December 1987. My wife Eunice and I then went home to live peacefully until the Lord took her to Himself on March 5, 2015. I very much appreciated her as my wife and friend. She kept the doors of our home open to many people and came with me to all my work stations."

Remelia enjoyed working with Bishop Wani as Wani was very good in pastoral work but not all that comfortable in administration. Remelia recalled his times with Bishop Wani. Remelia did all the office work, and enjoyed working with the clergy. He was able to solve many of their financial problems with their children in education, by providing salary advances from the Overseas Pastors' Children Fund.

Remelia is still thankful to God for the many things He did while he was the Bishop, including bringing together the revival groups in West Nile - the Strivers (CER) and the Pamusifu (The quiet ones). "My Bible verse which I wish to share with all is John 3:16 and my hymn is 60 in Alur: 'Anywogo Yesu Kristo Edoku Joriba' (I have found Jesus and he has become my Friend.) which is my message to the Christians of Madi and West Nile Diocese," he stated.

In Amin's time, Bishop Remelia was made the chairman of the allocation of the businesses of the departed Asians. He did it transparently, not allocating any shops to himself and discouraging people from coming to him secretly to get allocations.

Bishop Remelia Ringtho (left) and Archbishop Luwum

Bishop Remelia advised the clergy to build at least a small house at their home area and to prepare for retirement, but many clergy at the time were not happy with this.

Bishop Remelia remembered the time when the liberation army of the Tanzanians and Ugandan Guerilla groups advanced on Arua. Many frightened people left their homes and went into exile to the Democratic Republic of Congo and to Sudan. But he and his family, with Canon Maclure and his wife, Ven. Kezekia Ajule and Rev. Kefa Zoodia, the chaplain of Mvara Secondary School at the time, all chose to remain at Mvara.

When the liberators reached Arua, they went to Bishop Remelia's home and asked him, "Where is Idi Amin?" He told them that he did not know where Amin was. Then they asked him, "Why are you here?" He told them as a Bishop he was with his Christians.

The Tanzanian soldiers were good and kind to the people. But the Langi and Acholi soldiers would enter schools and colleges, including Arua Teachers' College, and loot things. When the Bishop was told about this, he came to the soldiers and asked them, "If they were liberators why should they loot things?" Then their commander told them to release the tutors and leave their property. The Bishop's home was a safe haven to many people who would bring their property to his home. One such person was Honourable Dick Nyai's mother who took her cattle to graze at the Bishop's compound.

Col. Sabiti, the army commander in Arua, told the Bishop to stay at Mvara. Each time the soldiers were troubling the people, the Bishop would go or write to Col. Sabiti and the people were usually helped. When a Leper called George at Muni was looted of all his cattle, he approached the Bishop who wrote to Col. Sabiti. George was taken to Ombaci to identify his cattle, which were given back.

The Christians at Mvara joined Bishop Remelia in morning prayers and sometimes soldiers also joined them. As long as the Christians were with the Bishop they were at peace, but not all. A lady called Joyce from Mvara, Kenya Zone, was shot by some soldiers when she resisted rape in her home. The saddest moment was when eight people: Member of Parliament Burua, Headmaster Gayo

Caka with his two sons, Lay Reader Yuda Bileti and four others were all shot dead at Muni and they were left to rot. Bishop Remelia went to Col. Sabiti and got permission to bury them, although they could only be identified by their shoes. Today a monument stands at Ewuata on the road to Muni NTC in memory of the eight.

In 1982, while Bishop Remelia was away in Pakwach, his own home was looted and some of his family fled to Warr. Remelia met them at Nebbi and took them to Warr, sending his driver back to fetch the rest of the family so that they could be together at Warr for the rest of the troubled time. The Catholic Bishop from Ediofe, Tarantino, also had to move to Warr when two Catholic Sisters at Ediofe were killed. The two bishops used to visit each other as they were living nearby.

Life was very hard during the war years as it was during Idi Amin's regime. Sugar was a luxury. People used to take tea without sugar. It was during this time when the the term "Ebede" came into use, saying "just get it there since the tea is without sugar." With all the insecurity and looting, people were not working in their gardens. Relief food was sent by the Church of Uganda Provincial office to the Diocese, but Bishop Remelia thought that this was just a short term solution. What the people needed was the means to produce their own food, so the Provincial office provided hoes and World Vision provided a lorry to distribute these to the Christians in the Diocese.

The Third Bishop of Madi West Nile Diocese: Bishop Ephraim Ewada Adrale 1988-1990
Ephraim Ewada Adrale was the last of eight children, born in 1935 to Matayo Ewada and Penina Ayiya at Anyavu village, Logiri, in Arua District. He joined Arua Primary School in 1944 and completed primary 6 before joining Arua Junior Secondary School. From 1954 to 1956 he was in Arua Teacher Training College and qualified as grade II teacher. In 1964 he became a headmaster

before joining Mukono Theological College to study for the Makerere University Diploma in Theology.

He married Salome Munduru in 1957 and she was later made Lay Canon of Emmanuel Cathedral in 2013. Bishop Adrale and Canon Salome had eight children. She went to be with her Lord, shortly after becoming a Canon.

Rev. Ephraim was ordained as Deacon in December 1974 and as priest in 1975 when he became Chaplain of Arua Teacher Training College. From July 1978 to 1981 he pursued further theological studies at Oak Hill College in the United Kingdom. While there, Ewada raised funds for the African Pastor Fund (now the African Pastors Fellowship) who provided brand new Raleigh bicycles for all the Church of Uganda pastors in the Madi and West Nile Diocese. "If you give us these old Raleigh Bicycles, to us they will be Mercedes Benzes," he said.

Bishop Ephraim Ewada Adrale

Ephraim Adrale returned from the UK, to be the Deputy Provincial Secretary for Refugees in the office of the Archbishop, a position he held until 1987 when he was elected 3rd Bishop of Madi West Nile Diocesan and consecrated in January 1988. He worked as Bishop till he went to be with the Lord on 13th February 1990.

It was Ephraim Adrale who planned the construction of the new Emmanuel Cathedral at Mvara; He strengthened ecumenism with other Christian churches particularly the Catholic Church headed by the then Bishop Frederick Drandua. As Bishop, he lobbied for better transport for the Diocesan Bishop and other staff, for the renovation of Arua Core PTC Chapel and other Diocesan infrastructure such as improvements in safe water coverage and improved hospital staff housing and hydroelectricity at Kuluva Hospital. He helped found Muni Girls' Secondary School, and helped to establish St. Luke's Dispensary and the Secondary School at Anyavu. While at Oak Hill College, as if God was preparing a succession plan, he lobbied for a scholarship for Caleb Mawa Nguma who eventually became his successor.

His great strengths lay in his humility, selflessness and trust. This helped him to make friends easily; his home was open to people of all tribes, race and strangers. Many top officials in the current government would attest to the education and welfare support he was able to give them when he was Deputy Provincial Secretary/Refugees in the Archbishop's office.

Bishop Ephraim Adrale's clean track record to reflect Christ in his service life was admired by his flock and the community. At his consecration and enthronement, Archbishop Yona Okot remarked, "Ephraim Adrale was so faithful in service to the extent he never was tempted to pick a penny from the vast resources he administered".

The Fourth Bishop of Madi West Nile Diocese: Bishop Caleb Ariaka Mawa 1990 - 1994

Bishop Caleb Mawa

Caleb Ariaka Mawa Nguma was born on 15th September, 1942 to Paul Nguma and Lucy Dravuru of Baito of Madi Okollo District. He married Janet Amukia Nguma in 1968. They were blessed with three boys and five girls and also raised several disadvantaged children. Caleb was educated at Jojoyi Primary School and Ombatini Secondary School, and then trained at the Central Government Prisons Staff College between 1964 and 1965. He further trained at Okollo Parish Training Center in 1970 before joining Bishop Tucker Theological College from 1972 to 1974.

He was ordained deacon on 9th February, 1975 and became a Priest on 23rd January, 1976. He served as a Chaplain at St. Aloysius College Nyapea until 1978 and then as Parish Priest, Arua Parish for a year. He then studied for a Diploma in Higher Education at Oak Hill Theological College, London, for a year and returned to serve as a Parish Priest in Arua Parish until 1985. He then studied for a two year MA at the Asian Centre for Theological Studies and Mission, returning to serve as Parish Priest for Ulepi, becoming Archdeacon for Madi Oyibu. In 1990, he went for an Advanced Leadership Training course in Singapore. When he came back he was elected as 4th Bishop Madi/West Nile Diocese in 1990 and was consecrated and enthroned on 3rd February, 1991.

Bishop Caleb was very instrumental in planning and collecting materials for the construction of the new Emmanuel Cathedral. Under him, development initiatives like the Bishop's farm were implemented; where different banana varieties were grown, a fish pond established and cattle raised. He was passionate about the spiritual, physical and economic development of the diocese. In conjunction with the Episcopal Church of South Sudan, he encouraged the establishment of Technical Colleges, Inde Technical Institute in Rhino Camp and Arua Vocational School at Diocesan HQ. He encouraged and promoted relationships with other Dioceses and white missionaries. He was mission-oriented and a good and passionate preacher.

Although he was very busy with Church ministry, Caleb was a family man and his family say he would always sing the family's favorite hymn, leading 'Ongo Nyiri' 60- "Ma ovu ayikosi asi mania" when he was with them. He also loved watching soccer.

He was on his way to meet the President for financial support to purchase the then Uganda Bookshop building on Transport Road as an investment for the diocese, when he was killed in a road accident.

The Fifth Bishop of the Madi and West Nile Diocese: Bishop Enock Drati Lee 1994-2005

Enock Lee Drati was born on October 27, 1939, in Lamila Village, Kijomoro Sub County in Maracha Distirct to Kurinalio Ajuni and Kezia Adroko. When he was nine, he went to Lamila Church of Uganda Village school and then lived with his uncle and attended P1-6 at Nyangilia Primary School in Koboko. He was baptized at Kamaka Church of Uganda in 1954 and confirmed by Bishop Keith Russell in Nyangilia Church of Uganda in Koboko Archdeaconry in 1956. He gave his life to Jesus Christ as his Lord and Savior in 1957. In 1957 he went to Mvara Junior Secondary School for two years and then to Sir Samuel Baker School in Gulu to complete his secondary education in 1961.

Enock Drati joined Uganda Prison Service in 1962 and served for seven years. He told of his experience while working as a Prison Warder, playing his accordion and reading his Bible openly to witness for Christ. Once, a white Prisons Officer insulted him, "Why do you stick to God?" Subsequently, he was laid off quietly from the prisons. Bishop Drati believes this was due to his stand for Christ.

He married Zillah in 1963 and they raised nine children. During his time in the prisons he studied in Emmaus Bible College by correspondence and obtained a Diploma in Biblical Studies and Christian Education in 1967. When he was laid off, he joined Bishop Tucker Theological College in Mukono for his ordination course from 1970 and was ordained deacon in 1972 and priest in 1973. He was posted as Chaplain and teacher to Moyo Secondary School, also serving at the Moyo Town Parish. While teaching at Moyo Secondary School, he took them to the national music competition, which the school won that year.

In 1975 Enock Drati went for further studies at Makerere University and obtained a Diploma in Music, Dance and Drama. While still a teacher at Moyo Secondary School, he got a place to study at Fuller Theological Seminary in Pasadena, California from 1978 to 1981. While he was at Fuller, he enrolled at

Azusa Pacific University and obtained BA degree in Religion and Philosophy in June 1981. At Fuller he completed his MA in Missiology in June 1982 and got his Doctor of Ministry (DMin) in June 1987. After his studies Enock Drati continued to live and work in a variety of roles in the USA, as a Missionary and Performing Artist, as an African Religious Writer, a Security Officer, as a Chaplain/Counsellor and in a Christian School.

In 1994 Drati Enock was consecrated the 5th Bishop of Madi/West Nile Diocese, where he served until 2005. He handed over to the 6th Diocesan Bishop Rt. Rev. Dr. Joel Obetia, after which he went back to the USA and served at St. Timothy Episcopal Church as a Chaplain and Teacher and at William Carey University in Pasadena and FAME World Wide as a Professor and Counselor until his death in 2011.

Bishop Drati worked hard all his life to expand the Kingdom of God in Uganda and abroad especially in the USA. He supported many families and friends to travel abroad, for education and these people became successful and God fearing. He also baptized and confirmed thousands of people both in Uganda and USA.

At the time Drati Lee became Bishop of Madi West Nile Diocese, the foundations of Emmanuel Cathedral were laid. He was instrumental in the building of the new Cathedral at Mvara, going out to raise funds for the construction. He also helped to expand study at Ringili for the Provincial Diploma in Theology to be a full campus of the Uganda Christian University. He is remembered for developing Kuluva Hospital Nurse Training School. It was during his time when "Here is Life", a local NGO, and DIGUNA, a German NGO, established the Voice of Life FM radio station.

Bishop Drati Lee

Dr. Drati became Bishop after the sudden deaths of both Bishop Adrale Ephraim and Bishop Caleb Ariaka Nguma. Many Christians attribute the power struggles within the Diocese to the shock of these deaths, leading to a lot of counter accusations, major challenges and divisions while Drati was leading the Diocese. Particularly in Arua Archdeaconry, the churches and parishes were heavily divided between the two camps of Dr. Drati and Venerable Draku. Bishop Drati did not have direct parish experience, which could partly explain the troubled times during his time in office. He had lived for 18 years in the USA and the clergy had an unrealistic expectation that money for their salaries and to solve the problems of the diocese would come from USA. Against this background a good number of the clergy were not loyal to Bishop Drati to the extent that many refused to accept transfers.

The Sixth Bishop of the Madi and West Nile Diocese: Bishop Joel Samson Obetia 2005-2017

Bishop Joel Samson Obetia was born on 17th May 1957 in Madi Okollo County in Arua District, Uganda to Samson Murua Drajoa and Susan Litriyi. He was baptized in 1969 and confirmed on 1974.

In 1972 Obetia joined Jojoyi Primary School, Madi Okollo and went to St Charles Lwanga College, Koboko to complete his Education in 1982. He enrolled for Evangelism and Discipleship Training at the Great Commission Training Centre (GCTC) in Nairobi, Kenya and from 1985 he became a National Staff Trainer for LIFE Ministry Uganda and GCTC.

Bishop Joel Obetia

He married Rev. Can. Joy Abia Kayeny Obetia in 1987 and they have five children. He became the Diocesan Mission Co-ordinator for Madi and West Nile from 1987 and from 1989 he coordinated the National Jesus Film activities for LIFE Ministry Uganda; this included preaching and training leaders. He also translated and lip-synched the Jesus Film into Lugbara. He returned to the role of Diocesan Mission Co-ordinator, Madi West Nile Diocese from 1993 to 1996.

In 1993, Obetia obtained his Bachelor of Divinity at Bishop Tucker Theological College, Mukono. While at Bishop Tucker College, he was Student's Minister for Campus Affairs, Editor of Evangelical Theology magazine and Mission and Evangelism Team Leader. He was ordained deacon on 1993 and priested in 1994.

In 1997 Joel Obetia graduated with a Masters degree in Mission and Ministry at Nottingham University, UK with a thesis on 'Worship as an Instrument of Mission in the Anglican Church of Uganda'. From 2002 to 2005, Obetia lectured in Practical Theology at Uganda Christian University Mukono. In 2008 he was awarded a Doctorate at Leeds University/Oxford Centre for Mission Studies with a thesis on 'Worship and Christian Identity in Uganda: A study of Contextualisation of Worship in the Anglican, Roman Catholic and Independent Churches of Uganda'.

Before becoming a Bishop, Joel Obetia served as the Chair of Governors of Okollo Secondary School, Arua, as the Chair of the Board of Mission, Madi West Nile Diocese and as a member of the Theology Commission of Uganda Joint Christian Council. On 27th November 2005 Bishop Joel was consecrated and enthroned as 6th Bishop of Madi/West Nile

From 2005 to 2016 Bishop Joel was the Chairman of the Theological and Ministerial Formation Commission, and from 2008 to 2014 he became a Member of the Uganda Christian University Council and Chairman from 2012 to 2016. From 2009 to 2016, he was the Chairman of the Constitutional Review Committee for Church of Uganda.

Much of his time in the early years of his leadership as Bishop was taken up with fire-fighting as the Drati-Draku divisions continued in the Diocese. Many are now grateful to God that Bishop Obetia was able to bring the two sides together and restore the unity of the Madi West Nile church. He has also been hugely influential in the World Church, serving as a Bishop for GASCOM, the Global South Provinces for the Anglican Communion.

The Seventh Bishop of the Madi and West Nile Diocese: Bishop Charles Collins Andaku   2017 -
Bishop Charles Collins Andaku, known to many as a humble educationist and mentor, was born on 22nd November, 1965, the first of ten children of Rev. Canon Semi Draku and Rachel Draku of Kibigoro Village, Katrini Sub-county, Terego County in Arua District. Bishop Andaku recalls moving as a child from one church to another as his father's role changed until his retirement as Archdeacon. Most of his early life was spent at Emmanuel Cathedral at Mvara, where his father was the parish priest.

"I was baptized in 1966, confirmed in October 1976, married in the Church on 20th February 1993 and above all Born Again on 10th August 1984 in a Scripture Union Conference at Mvara Secondary School. The Lord touched my heart after a long battle and struggle with my own life. Although I had lived in the pastor's house, went to Sunday School, participated in Scripture Union and youth programs, I never committed my life to Jesus as my Lord and Saviour, remaining a nominal Christian. After my primary education at Ombokoro Primary School and secondary level at Mvara SS, I trained as a secondary school teacher at Muni National Teachers College in 1991-1992."

He received a Bachelor of Education from Makerere University in 1999 and Master of Divinity from Uganda Christian University in 2009. While at UCU Andaku was the chairperson of the Christian Union and a student chaplain.

Bishop Andaku says, "I am married to Jane Andaku, a primary school head teacher. Jane is a daughter of the late Archdeacon Daniel Govile and we are blessed with a son called Emmanuel Sydney Draku, who graduated from

Makerere University. My wife and our son are born again. They love and care for me and above all they are a source of comfort and encouragement in my pastoral ministry. I want to testify to the goodness of the Lord for giving me the grace to cleave to my beloved wife Jane for 23 years despite many discouraging threats from people based on traditional belief that a woman is to produce as many children as possible which has not been the case with us."

He was ordained deacon in special ordination ceremony in July 2005 by Rt. Rev. Dr Enoch Lee Drati at Emmanuel Cathedral Mvara and in August 2006 ordained priest at Emmanuel Cathedral Mvara by Rt. Rev. Dr Joel Obetia. In 2010, he was posted back as Chaplain to Muni Girl's Secondary School and in 2012 transferred to Emmanuel Cathedral Mvara as vicar. On May 1, 2016 he was made a Canon in the Diocese of Madi and West Nile by Rt. Rev. Dr Joel Obetia.

Bishop Charles Collins Andaku was consecrated and enthroned as the 7th Bishop of Madi and West Nile Diocese on 26th February 2017 at Emmanuel Cathedral. The theme for his charge was taken from 1 John 4:7:

"Let us love one another." This reflects his commitment to embracing the diversity and spirit of dialogue that heals and inspires unity in the Body of Jesus Christ. Many refer to Bishop Andaku as the Centenary Bishop as the Diocese celebrates the 100 years of the existence of the Anglican Church in West Nile climaxing on June 24th 2018.

Archbishop Ntagali shows the new Bishop Andaku to the congregation

In 1993, what was the Goli Archdeaconry of Madi West Nile Diocese became the new Diocese of Nebbi, with Henry Orombi as the first Bishop of Nebbi.

Bishop Henry Luke Orombi the first Bishop of the Nebbi Diocese
Henry Luke Orombi is an Alur of Jonam from Pakwach, born on 11th October 1949, the fifth child out of eleven of Luka Jalobo and Susan. His name Orombi simply means *'Gather together and fill the place'*. He went to Pajobi Primary School in the 1950's at the age of eight and the Bible was his favorite book. He hated Mathematics but never missed an English lesson. As he grew up he developed an interest in education, becoming a school prefect, a time keeper and a school debater. He frequently attended Bible study taught by the catechists every Thursday, becoming an excellent Bible verse reciter particularly Psalms.

As a teenager, Orombi loved to link up with his uncle Wilson the herdsman, who told thrilling stories, or to go boating and fishing in the River Nile, to evade school attendance but Luka, his father, encouraged him to concentrate on school. Marrying early, as his culture demanded, would end up with a bleak future. His father's words stung him so hard that he lost interest in the cultural privileges. He was given everything he needed to perfect his studies, reading extremely hard and managing to obtain grade one in P6 to be admitted in a Junior Secondary School.

In February 1966 Luka and some of Orombi's teachers all encouraged him to become a school teacher. But Orombi had no wish to teach in the classroom, his ambition was to become a motor cycle mechanic like the famous Ramathan in Pakwach, who rode motor cycles at terrific speed, and to train at Elgon Technical School in Mbale District. But his father resisted this choice and took him to Arua Primary Teachers College, persuading the staff to include Orombi on the interview list. Orombi prayed inwardly to fail the interview to give him a green light to become a mechanic, but God turned him down.

Orombi passed the test highly and was enrolled there and then at the College to train as a grade II teacher against his will. His joyous father hurried home to fetch all his things. Orombi gave in to his father's pressure and became a good friend to the Principal of the Teacher Training College, Stewart Cole and his wife May. He still disliked Cole's subject, Mathematics, but liked his Music and appreciated May for teaching his favorite subject English.

While a student he played basketball and irregularly drank strong alcohol with friends but fellowshipped with the other students during Scripture Union hours. On March 22 1967, Orombi had a sleepless night. He woke up, knelt down and welcomed Jesus Christ into his life. His dormitory mates never expected it and couldn't believe that he had become a *mulokole* when he told them the following morning. At home during holidays, Mama Susan welcomed Orombi's new faith, she had expected him to follow. The born again student was surprised to learn that his mother had prior knowledge of his faith. Orombi loved Jesus Christ with all his heart. When he returned to college his friends expected him to abandon his faith.

In third year, the determined Orombi got elected into the office of vice president to lead Students' government and that same year was elected Chairperson of Scripture Union. He loved to read the Bible and spear-head SU activities, balancing leadership with studies and preparing himself for school practice. The following year Orombi became Male Head Student and made friends with students who had received Jesus Christ as their personal Saviour.

A Lugbara lady called Rose, who became the Female Head student, won Orombi's admiration. He wrote a letter to her to seek her love, but she was already in relationship with the Sudanese national Wilberforce Vundru, who was his friend. In her reply she accepted Orombi, but requested him not to disclose the affair to Vundru. But as Orombi and Vundru were intimate friends, Orombi showed him the letter and the two laughed aloud. Vundru surrendered Rose to Orombi and urged him to test her love in marriage and he proposed her to be his partner.

In 1968, the Scripture Union leaders were invited to Gayaza High School in Kampala, to teach senior four and senior six leavers how to reach the world, to serve other Christians and to share the word of God. Rose, the friend of Orombi, also attended the conference and the two laid strategies to establish a home through the church. The young couple planned to reach out to their families in Pakwach and Arua for introductions but couldn't make it because in 1970 Orombi was deployed to teach in Lira district while Rose remained within Arua. Due to the long distance between Orombi and Rose, their relationship became a nightmare.

In 1971 the Chaplain of Canon Lawrence Teacher's College urged Orombi to join the Ministry of God. Although the young teacher turned down the request, the Chaplain informed the Bishop of Northern Uganda Diocese that Orombi should have a place in the Bishop Tucker Theological College in Mukono, because he thought Orombi had the capabilities to become a church leader. As older Christians in Lira also saw in Orombi a good seed to germinate into a priest, Bishop Janani Luwum of Northern Uganda interviewed Orombi for a place at Bishop Tucker College, but without success.

One Sunday afternoon Orombi needed some charcoal to do cooking. He went to a grass-thatched Anglican church, where the congregation was still in the church for service at 2pm, and sat on the back bench. Pastor David who saw him, welcomed him to be part of the fellowship and asked the visitor to say a word. Orombi stood up and introduced himself as the Deputy Head Teacher of Ambalal primary school, revealing that he was a born again Christian who confessed Christ in 1967. He said he never came to pray but to look for some charcoal. After the church service, Pastor David and Orombi had tea with cassava in his home. The Pastor secured some charcoal and Orombi bought it. Pastor David encouraged him to visit him at home and the two men soon became great friends. Each time Orombi felt lonely or bored, he immediately sought Pastor David at his home to share light moments with laughter and prayed to overcome challenges. Their bond became stronger.

While Orombi's dreams of becoming a priest hovered around, he needed a partner to bring an end to his bachelor life. He went to his uncle Elia Topacho with a bag of his favorite potatoes. Topacho inquired if Orombi was married and he answered no because he had no resources to keep a wife and he had the responsibility to pay for his siblings. Topacho then promised to foot all the wedding expenses if he could find a lady to marry soon. The grateful young man was so excited he could not sleep. He wrote a letter to Rose to remind her of their relationship but Rose was engaged to somebody already.

After further unfruitful meetings in Lira, Orombi was back in Pakwach when Lydia his niece gave him some good news, but the girl meant for him was not at home. When the girl known as Phoebe returned she was told about a tall, energetic, intelligent, gentle man with light skin complexion, who wanted her hand in marriage. Phoebe knew that this was Orombi who had taught her in P5.

Phoebe was born in Goli in Zombo district in November 1954 and became a born again Christian in 1971. She was rejected by her father and decided to live with her mother, but was never able to continue with her studies as her father stopped paying her school fees when he learnt that she was a *molokole*. Several years later when Mama Phoebe was forty nine, she passed her O Level Certificate and took a Certificate and a Diploma in counseling at Kampala School of Theology. Girls whose education was interrupted heard of her success story and resumed schooling. "If Phoebe went back to school, why not they themselves?" they asked.

On June 3rd 1972 Orombi and Phoebe walked to the altar and took marriage vows. Orombi could not believe that he had found a wife who swore to be his beloved till death in spite of having no time to date her. Their wedding day was attended by just a few guests and cost only 40 shillings to buy some rice and a goat. The brief reception was under a tree and the couple disappeared as soon as eating was over for their honeymoon at Chobe Safari Lodge at Murchison Falls National Park. Orombi believes their marriage is a special one from God's Kingdom in Heaven, because their courtship never lasted for days for them to learn each other thoroughly yet it worked. They moved to Lira where Orombi continued with his teaching career. They celebrated their 40 years of married life on June 3rd 2012.

The following Saturday, June 10th 1972 Orombi and Phoebe met her Pentecostal friends in the little church. That particular day, Lodoviko Owino, the associate Pastor, preached about the Holy Spirit baptism, but Orombi's heart sank. He thought it was the worst subject his bride could learn from the Pentecostals. Fortunately Owino preached well and called for anyone who wanted to receive the Holy Spirit to stand up. Everybody stood up except Orombi and Phoebe the true Anglicans, who prayed silently. The Holy Spirit came upon Orombi and with his wife he began to speak in strange tongues. Orombi rose to his feet and gave his testimony. "Hallelujah!" screamed the congregation while they jumped up and down.

> *Loving Jesus glory be to you!*
> *I love you Lord,*
> *Jesus gave power,*
> *Jesus gave me peace,*
> *Jesus gave me joy.*

In late August, Orombi was invited to speak at a conference for Scripture Union groups in Gulu. He spoke about the Samaritan woman in the Gospel of John 4:1-6, and was touched by the Spirit of God when he taught them a song he had composed. The youth sang it well with drums and shakers, bringing liveliness to the conference. Orombi called upon believers in the Lord Jesus Christ to surrender their lives to Him and without hesitation, 250 converts came forward.

Orombi could not believe that such number of youth could turn to Christ. He repeated the call to Christ to ensure that there was no doubt as *Balokole* but the same number rose to prove that they were determined to be with Jesus Christ, including an American Catholic nun. Orombi never expected such a massive response and it became rather difficult for the counsellors to handle the newly born agains. At the end each counsellor had to minister to 40-50 converts.

In 1972 Orombi was appointed as the deputy head teacher of Ambalal Primary School, but some teachers thought he was too young to lead a school and not a native of Lango. When the head teacher left to become District Education Officer, he recommended that Orombi take over the school, but he hesitated, thinking that he has God's Gospel about the risen Lord to share with young people in schools and in parishes. But the DEO persuaded Orombi to take the responsibility until someone could be found to replace him. Orombi accepted the post and gradually came to like the job. He related well with his staff and loved his pupils but was still dedicated to preaching the Word of God.

It was Bishop Janani Luwum, who heard Orombi preaching at Kitgum High School and was impressed by Orombi's potential, leading him into priesthood. Orombi wanted to be a Church Army Captain, and said no to Bishop Luwum but the high ranking clergy requested him to join Bishop Tucker Theological College in Mukono to become ordained. Orombi still resisted this call. But while at St. Andrews Guest House at the Diocesan Headquators in Mbale town and reading Ezekiel Chapter 8, Orombi clearly heard the voice of God calling him to join the church, as if somebody stood behind him. Orombi gave up his working life to the most gracious God and abandoned the teaching profession.

When Sunday came, Odur, his preaching partner learnt of his intention to quit teaching with good pay to live a miserable life without coins in his pockets, he tried to dissuade him but the determined Orombi stood his ground. In 1973 Orombi resigned from Lango District Administration Education Department and gave way to serve God by boarding a train for Pakwach with Phoebe and their baby girl Helen. They arrived at Pakwach, with half of the luggage stolen. In 1974, the family moved again to Gulu district where Orombi worked as a lay evangelist, the Assistant Education Secretary and the Assistant Youth Secretary for the diocese. They had little money but were given firewood and fresh ground nuts and some kind Christians gave them monthly savings. The family survived till God's plan worked for them. The church ministry and their family grew. Helen was born in 1973 in Lira and Bob born in 1974 in Gulu, in the year that

Janani Luwum became the Archbishop of Uganda, Rwanda, Burundi and Boga-Zaire.

Orombi joined Bishop Tucker Theological College to take the Makerere University Diploma in Theology. On Feb. 17 1977 he heard the shocking news about the death of Bishop Janani Luwum with two cabinet ministers, Oboth Ofumbi and Lt. Col. Erinayo Oryema, who were all said to have perished in a car accident. But the naked fact revealed that Bishop Janani died of gunshot in the mouth by Idi Amin. After these deaths, Orombi went to the College Principal to quit the course in protest at Bishop Janani's death. He was given three days to review his decision. He packed his bag with his belongings, picked up his guitar and left Mukono. There God revealed the vision of Jonah who escaped aboard a ship from delivering the word of God to Nineveh, but ran away to Tarshish. Orombi saw himself as Jonah fleeing to be God's ambassador. He returned, to finish his training in December 1978. In January 1979, Orombi was ordained deacon and was deployed as Madi and West Nile Diocesan Youth Officer.

In May 1980, Orombi was given a scholarship by Holy Trinity Church Brompton, the home of the Alpha Course that is taught in many churches, to spend three years in the UK. Orombi was then appointed as Archdeacon of Goli Archdeaconry. He shifted his family to Goli and found the Archdeacon's headquarters in a dilapidated state and repaired it. Visiting the 24 parishes in the Archdeaconry, he preached the word of God about evangelism, stewardship, time management, nutrition and basic health care, and acquired a new Land Rover for the church with loud speakers to spread the message about God.

In Feb.1993 Orombi was elected the First Bishop Archbishop Henry Orombi of Nebbi Diocese and was consecrated on Oct. 24th 1993. On July 4th 2003 Orombi was elected the 7th Archbishop of the church of Uganda at Hannington Chapel in Namirembe at the age of 55. He replaced Archbishop Livingstone Mpalanyi-Nkoyoyo.

In 1989, Orombi organized a convention in Nebbi which was attended by 600 people and 450 of them accepted Jesus Christ as their personal Saviour. In the same year, Orombi and Phoebe were invited to the USA and while there, they met John Paul Jackson of Vineyard Church, Los Angeles, who spoke eight prophetic words into Orombi's life. While he was the Bishop of Nebbi, Orombi established a training center and pioneered the establishment of a Prayer Mountain, now a very popular retreat centre in West Nile. During the 1998 Lambeth Conference, Orombi was among the 800 Anglican Bishops and 30 Archbishops who were invited by Queen Elizabeth II to take tea with her. She invited them in her capacity as the Defender of the Faith and Supreme Governor of the Church of England .

Retired Archbishop Henry Luke Orombi

Orombi's Christian work in proclaiming the word of God has been recognized internationally through the Kairo's Journal Award ceremony in New York where he won $25,000, which he used to renovate the dilapidated Provincial Offices. While on a Gospel mission to Singapore, God heard Orombi's prayers and the Archbishop of Singapore raised $20,000, and to carry on the renovation work in Kampala. In 2007 Orombi again attended the Kairo's Journal Award ceremony in New York. He met Rev. Can. Patrick Sookdeo of Barnabas Fund who gave him $134,000 to finish the renovation of the Provincial Offices.

His work in reconciliation led to him being invited to America again to discuss the problems that affect Northern Uganda with Senators. He has met both the Rwandan President Paul Kagame and the Eritrean President Isasias Afwerki. Orombi went to China in 2011, invited by the Chinese government who wanted the church in the Global South in Latin America, Africa and Asia to meet with both the Chinese government officials and church officials. The Chinese yearned for the word of God and Orombi returned home with a heart to pray for the Chinese.

Later that year, Orombi met the Anglican bishops for a retreat together with 32 Pentecostal pastors and Anglicans to seek repentance and apologies between the two denominations. They were reconciled and forgave each other with hugging and tears of joy. In August 2011 Orombi officiated at the event to choose President Museveni's daughter Natasha Museveni Karugire as the girl child education patron in Nebbi diocese. Natasha was chosen to bridge the gap between northern and southern parts of the nation together.

In Uganda, many have commented on Orombi's straightforward approach, a man of God who calls a spade a spade and does not compromise. They appreciate his humility and ability to get on with everybody, his passion for Youth Ministry and support for Scripture Union, his gifts as a preacher and ability to mobilize young people to serve the Church. As a pastor, mentor and shepherd, he has brought many to Christ. Canon John Yobuta Ondoma simply describes Orombi as his best friend, whom he first met as a student at Arua T.T.C. in 1966. 'Our friendship has continued till today…. He values people and cares for them heartily. He lives and practices his faith sincerely. He is a person whose friendship I value and would like to cherish.'

After the election of Henry Orombi to be Archbishop, **Bishop Alphonse Wathokodi became the second and current Bishop of the Nebbi Diocese.**

Chapter 7
The Revival Movement in West Nile
By Dr Enzama Wilson and Canon Ondoma John

1. **Introduction**

This chapter provides insights into the history of the East African Revival (EAR) and the experiences of early converts in West Nile. Today a good number of Christians are saved and members of revival fellowships across West Nile but do not know when and how revival movement started and came to West Nile. Besides, others do not understand the features of revival as was coined and promoted at the beginning of the movement. Many of the original features of revival have been undermined by the changing social, cultural and spiritual environment and modernization. Evangelism and soul winning which were the aspirations of the EAR have become the core mission of the church.

Today we see the revivalists working very well with the church and in fact it was incorporated into the diocese as a unit under the department of Mission and evangelism. We now see all priests and clergy and their spouses and many Christians saved. But this was not so in the beginning of revival. The early converts in West Nile were tortured by the local government and church leaders for confessing Christ as their personal Saviour and Lord.

A lot has been written on the history of EAR in Uganda, but there is scanty information on the revival movement and experiences of the early balokole in West Nile. The little knowledge has been obtained from oral testimonies of early converts. This chapter attempts to fill this gap.

It is drawn from the testimonies and experiences of some of the early revivalists who are still alive. These include Tefolo Debo (one of the members persecuted by the church for embracing revival), Baranabas Avinyia, Baba Remelia Ringtho (retired bishop), Paineto Obia (renowned reawakened fellowship member). We also had informal conversations with a number of contemporary revivalists, who gave their perceptions and experiences as well. The church and revivalists operated like opponents in the mission field.

2. Revival Touches Ground in West Nile

The epicentre of revival movement in Uganda was known to be in central Uganda. The East African Revival was brought to West Nile by Dr. Eliya Lubulwa in 1949. Lubulwa had become a Mulokole in the early 1940s in Kampala at a time when some of the early converts started to compromise their belief. He castigated them in his fiery preaching style, using a local megaphone which he had made from an old paraffin tin. Lubulwa eventually disagreed with William Nagenda who was the leader of the revival in Buganda. In his view, the revival movement was losing its steam and becoming lukewarm. He argues for the balokole to strive to be pure. Later his group of radical balokole were known as Strivers while the rest were East African Revivals. Dr. Lubulwa was transferred to Kitgum in 1947 and where Justo Otunnu and Janan Luwumu were converted.

In 1949, Lubulwa was transferred from Kitgum to Moyo as a doctor. In Moyo he made converts. One of them was Sosteni Ajuku, a teacher, who brought his radical preaching, the Striver type of balokole, to northern Uganda. Ajuku and the other converts followed his style of open air mission, preaching with the use of local trumpets. Eventually, this group were known as Trumpeters. The focus of the revival message was on sin and repentance, Cross, baptism of the spirit, sanctification and the continual desire to pursue holiness. Conversion was an overwhelming experience of brokenness at the foot of the Cross, which required public confession of sins. Prior to the revival movement, Christian experiences were not recognized as "*asi ojaza*"-being saved.

Baranabas Avinyia recalls that, later when the Daudi Asendu and other new converts went for a conference in Kampala, they discovered that, the balokole in Buganda were not as radical as Lubulwa and Ajuku were making the West Nilers to believe. Many of them started to work closely with the church. They were called Pamuzifu. Most of the elites such as Samson Avua, Baranaba Avinyia,

Babanga, Alidri etc, who got saved as students in Mvara Junior, were members of Pamuzifu. This is where the division in the revival movement in West Nile began. The strivers would use their trumpets to disrupt church services by preaching on the church premises, sometimes, when the service is in progress, or immediately when service is over.

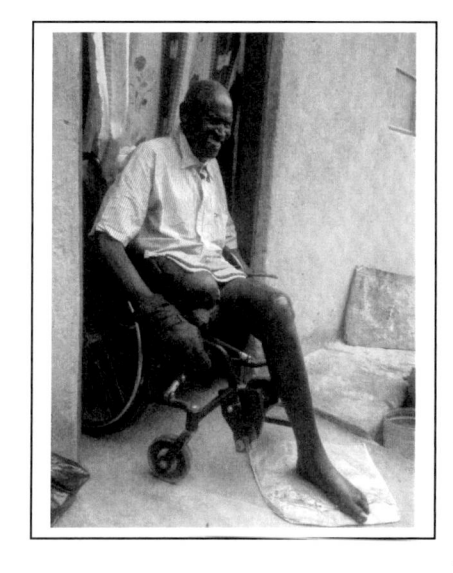

One of the prominent leader to emerge was Tefolo Debo, who got saved in 1959, ten years later. Surprisingly the day Tefolo got converted it was not revivalists who preached to him but an Area Leader (lay reader) in a funeral service in Lamila, Maracha District, at the age of 29. This means, although some of the church leaders did not approve of the revival openly, they were practicing and preaching salvation. Tefolo would later become diocesan revival leader after Ajuku. Later Tefolo abandoned the Striver style and joint the church loyalists.

Tefolo Debo

It should be noted that, in the early years of revival, the church leaders were not saved. Indeed, many of the priests and lay readers were still practicing their previous way of life, including growing and smoking of tobacco and drinking of alcohol. Baba Remilia, observed that, Bishop Silvanus Wani, was one of the first priests to be saved. This gave the revivalists in his parish impetus to influence church administration. The revivalists castigated priests and lay readers who were not converted. They could request Bishop Wani to transfer Lay Readers they felt were not opening doors for the gospel. This practice started to cause division in the church, rather than provide ground for the church to grow.

3. The revival message gains ground

The more the revivalists had public preaching opportunities, the more their message appealed to the listeners. The difference between the church's way of operation and that of the revivalists:

(a) The church leaders were not reaching to the people. Instead, the people came to the church, where the leaders were. The new discourse of the revivalists was to reach out to the people, where they were, that is, market squares, work places, schools, hospitals. In this way, people's problems were addressed at the point of their need. The people began to see the revival message as an alternative and not complementary to the missionary message.

(b) The revivalist discourse emphasized the transforming power of the Gospel and renewal of the Holy Spirit in the lives of those who repent and believe. They emphasized "newness and change that attracts converts. The saved ones feel completely different and their habits and attitudes were changed toward resisting evil and striving to good".

(c) Many people marvelled at the courage of these men and women, many of whom were unschooled but would take on the, otherwise "feared" white district administrators without fear. Even when they were being threatened and jailed, they would not relent. This also disturbed the leaders the more, because, they were not sure of where and how these men got courage from. But of course, the missionaries were aware that these men were preaching the biblical truths of the gospel.

Tefolo contends that, it reached a point where if an issue was to be presented from the diocese to the congregations, the Christians would ask if this had been sanctioned by the revival leaders. Because they knew, if it was not, then this was not a good thing in which Christians should participate. In general, revivalists started to set the pace and standards for the church growth.

4. Friction between the Revivalist and church leaders
The early balokole in West Nile such Ajuku, Tefolo, Asendu and others faced stiff opposition from the church. Baba Remilia and Tefolo recall that, many of these fellows were put in jail. Ajuku was jailed several times with hard labour by the government, often at the request of the missionaries, to deter him and others

from being 'public nuisance'. Ajuku was asked to choose between being a teacher and revival. It was reported, that he chose both. He argued that teaching was a source of livelihood while winning souls was responding to the call of the great Commission. He was then relieved of his duty as a teacher.

Tefolo was imprisoned five times for his open-air service and for winning souls for Christ. However, the prison experience made revivalist more vigilant as they would compare their experience to that of the early church movement of Paul and Peter. Tefolo observes that, their driving force was to see the world saved but not any material or financial benefits as the case would be. The following were some of reason the church was against revival:

The method of operation: The radical way of spreading the Gospel in public places, market squares, office compounds. To be heard by the public, the Strivers made local trumpets (known as guka) as public-address systems. The use of guka brought in a new dimension in the revival movement. The guka-wielding converts were eventually known as the Northern Trumpeters. This irked many government and church leaders in the districts because they disturbed public peace and were considered a nuisance. Besides, the use of guka was attracting people to these revivalists in large number.

Lack of training: The church argued that these revivalists were not trained in theology or Bible studies, therefore, they did not have authority to preach the Gospel in the first place. They feared these people would preach messages contrary to that of the missionaries. While for the missionaries, it was argued by some respondents, the messages of the revivalists would soon override principles of the Church of Uganda and many African church leaders would soon reject their (missionaries) authority and embrace the new-found life changing messages from revival movement. This would undermine their authority and power in the eyes of the Christians.

The revival gaining ground: One of the things that irked the church leaders was the fact that revivalist movement was taking root faster than they anticipated.

The revivalists were dangerously courageous and brutally frank. The principle of changed life was what endeared the revival message to the public. While the message of the missionaries did not bring change in the way of life of the Christians and church leaders, the message of revival emphasized changed life- repentance from many habits and practices such as no more drinking of alcohol, no polygamy, no smoking and a number of habits and practices that need to be abandoned for the sake of the Gospel. The public started to see changes in the lives of the converts and many were curious to know the source of and to experience these changes.

Public confessions: The principle of public confession, repentance and restitution caused problems with the church because converts would confess sins such as having sexual intercourse with a cow, both women and men would confess of masturbation, how they were able to corner girls and for women how they managed to seduce men to have sexual intercourse with them. This was, to the church leaders, tantamount to obscene talk in the church in the presence of boys and girls. It would open ground to the youth to practice some of the tricks other than refraining from doing them, which was the intention of the converts.

As a result, the church started to sanction the revival fellowships because some of the teachings were against the social norms of the society and church principles, while causing division in the families. Converted spouses whose parftners were not saved were regarded by them as devils in the home. Some were teaching against paying bride price, paying of *avu ti*, (a cow paid to the maternal uncles of a deceased person). Many other such social and traditional practices were regards as satanic. Revival members should not put on neck ties, coats, not style their hair and women should not go to the salon, women should not wear trousers etc. Mr. Ajuku for example stopped playing his guitar because guitars were symbols of night clubs to which revivalist no longer went.

5. The impact of Revival Messages to the Anglican Church in West Nile
As the revival movement started to take root and spread all over the region, and many Christians started to get saved and practice the principle of the EAR

movement, the church began to realize the impacts of the revival message. First of all, this would become one of the values the revival movement added to the church. The church began to grow steadily in both numbers and commitment to biblical and spiritual values as more people started to dig deep into the Bible, where they were able to understand the movement from biblical perspective and not humanly.

Secondly, due to the teaching of the revival, the church offerings started to increase as Christians recognized giving as part of worship and commitment. The remuneration of the pastors started to increase. That is when the church started to embrace the revival movement. It became the lifeline of the church as we know today. Revival movement in the church today appears the "fuel" for the spiritual growth of the church.

Thirdly, many of the converted educated Christians such as teachers, began to receive calls for ordained ministry as tent makers, who would be posted as chaplains to the mushrooming schools around the region. That explains the many priests from the teaching profession, those days.

6. Different factions of revival movement in West Nile

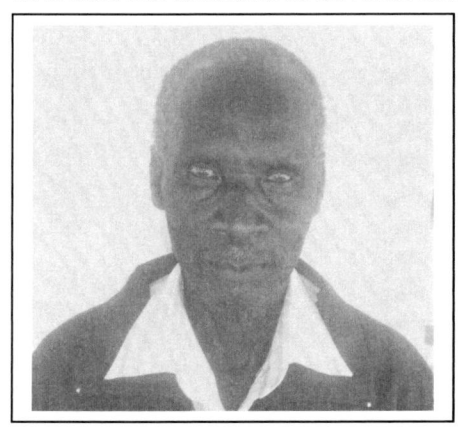

Yoram Sarua, CER Leader

In 1970, the Strivers metamorphosed into Chosen Evangelical Revival (CER) with connections to Justo Otunu from Acholi and Ajuku from West Nile. Later after the death of Ajuku, Tefolo Debo took over until he joined the Church of Uganda Revival and became its leader, leaving CER to be headed by Yoram Sarua up to date. The two groups despite Bishop Wani trying to bring them together in 1970s have remained separate, but not fighting each other.

When Bishop Lee Drati became bishop, he gave opportunity for the CER to return to the church if they were willing. Quite a good number returned to the church. The church began confirming and baptizing their children, they were allowed to take part in Holy Communion etc. However, many of the members of the CER did not join the revival fellowship and conferences organized by the CoU Revival. In other words, they joined the church but not the revival fellowship in the church, preferring to hold their own fellowships, till this day.

The Church of Uganda Revival leadership has moved from Tefolo Debo to Rev. Gard Uriama and now to Samuel Ondia. But CER leadership has remained in the hands of Yoram Sarua, with their Secretary being Rev. Johnson Andama, the University Secretary for Uganda Christian University Arua Campus. Although revival movement was brought to West Nile by an educated Muganda, the leadership of the two revival groups in West Nile has largely been in the hands of unschooled members. But this has not deterred the growth of the movement as we see today.

7. Quest for a new revival

The emergency of the charismatic renewal movement was appealing to the young and educated. But the church sees that young people are now rejecting counsel from their elders, refusing to follow the conservative values of the East African Revival, even if they consider themselves as saved and experiencing evangelistic principles. As a result, at present, the revival movement is seen as a movement for the old fellows which is gradually giving way to a new form of revivalism, anchored on spirit focused rather than cross-centred Christian life.

8. Conclusion

Revival movement was formed in 1936 in Rwanda and spread quickly to the whole of East Africa. The EAR reached West Nile after thirteen years of its existence. By then the church in West Nile was already 31 years old, already entrenched in its principles and with trained native church leaders to manage its affairs.

We have seen that the church and the population did not fully understand the mission of the Holy Spirit through the revival movement thus leading to persecuting them for their evangelistic activities and soul winning mission. On the other hand, the revivalists were too bold and frank that it was not easy for people to understand the source of their boldness and what was driving them into these actions. They were easily labelled as crazy lot of fellows.

The good news is that, today salvation has taken root in every church and church leaders have embraced the revival spirit. The revival has set the spiritual standards and principles for the development and growth of the church in West Nile.

Two Footnotes to this account of Revival in West Nile:

1. **Kevin Ward** wrote an account of the Revival across East Africa and the following provides a useful appendix to the section above:

'West Nile has a distinctive church life of its own, largely because it was evangelized not by CMS but by the Africa Inland Mission, working as part of the Native Anglican Church. The initial attitude of AIM to the Revival was one of suspicion, more especially as they met it first in Lubulwa's aggressive variety. With a rather more paternalist attitude than CMS, AIM was less likely to welcome a movement inspired so strongly by local initiative.

In Kenya AIM was to reject the Balokole revival, partly because it was so closely identified with the Anglican Church. But in Uganda, where the AIM was working under the Anglican Church, there developed a rather more favourable attitude, especially after some of the missionaries working in West Nile were deeply touched by the impact of staying at Namutamba and attending the 1949 Kako Convention. This led to rather stronger backing for the Revival in West Nile than CMS missionaries gave in other parts of the diocese of Upper Nile.

West Nile Christianity has thrived under the impact of the Revival - indeed the experience of West Nile is more that of Kigezi than any other area in northern Uganda. But the Revival has been divided between the Trumpeters and the Church of Uganda Revival. In 1976 Bishop Wani managed to effect a reconciliation which harnessed the whole Revival movement in the service of the Church. But the bitter experiences of war in West Nile in the early 1980s, personality conflicts among the Balokole exile in Sudan, and the influence of Otunu's CER from Acholi, have combined to make the reconciliation seem fragile at times.

2. **Rev Canon Manoah Ofuta has written a moving account of the suffering of early supporters of Revival**:

The early missionaries introduced the local converts to reading the Bible through Bible Classes and using the printed Bible passages. One could only be baptized if he/she knew how to read the Bible. The Missionaries' aim was to build Christians in the word of God and thus know the true God and resist the devil. The Christians read about God and Jesus Christ and Holy Spirit which paved the way to salvation.

When the East African Revival made its way to West Nile, it already found Christians who were searching the Scriptures. The Christians did not have to depend on the Church leaders for their spiritual growth, they discovered the truth from the Bible reading and the Holy Spirit gave them the new birth and insight. Many Christians became converts (Abalokole) because the Bible opened their eyes to see the salvation

Life was not easy for the Christians who wanted to apply what they read from the Bible. Many took the word of the Scriptures literally. Many Abalokole saw the different lives the missionaries and African Church leaders lived. The Abalokole started opposing them openly. After Sunday services, the members of the revival would gather by the church door and challenge the missionaries and church leaders why they did not get saved and confess their sins.

This brought conflict between the Abalokole and the missionaries and African Church leaders. This led to persecution of the Abalokole. Many Abalokole were beaten, and thrown into prison. The following are some of the Abolokole who suffered most: Ajuku Sosetence, Esita Okia, Rebeka Kilaa, Ludia Timaru. One member of the revival who then was youthful, Tephelo Debe was made to break six ant hills a day. He broke the anthills but they never broke his spirit in the Lord. Later he became a towering leader of the revival in West Nile.

Persecution of the Christians who were calling people to live the life the Bible tells continued to spread: local church leaders persecuted the members of their congregations who preached in the open air by the church compounds. Husbands persecuted their wives who attended fellowship meetings, conferences and conventions. Some wives were made to look at the sun with their naked eyes. Some were sent out of their houses. One example is Mary Orotroa who slept with her children in Emmanuel Church in Mvara; fathers persecuted their children who got saved and witnessed to them using the Bible verses they had read.

Teaching to read the Bible from printed material produced only Bible readers. They depended wholly on what they read from the Bible. One set back on making the ability to read the Bible as a condition before becoming a Christian and receiving Baptism was that those who wanted to join the Anglican Church but could not read the Bible and therefore could not be baptized, left the Anglican Church to remain in traditional religions or joined the Roman Catholic Church or joined Islam.

Chapter 8
The Growth of Ministries within the Church

8.1 Mothers' Union
by Hellen Enzama, Canon Sally Anguyo and Philister Bileti

Mothers Union members lining up for a service

What is Mothers' Union?
Mothers' Union is an international organization within the Anglican Communion, in which members believe in the importance of families as well as encouraging and supporting families and marriages. Members work to reach out as God's family to those who are isolated, in trouble or in need of help.

Mothers' Union was established by Mrs. Mary Elizabeth Summer in 1876 in England. Mary's vision was to encourage parents in caring for their children not just physically and mentally, but also spiritually. From the onset it was recognized that strong relationships defined the role of the family, that these relationships were crucial in building healthy communities. Mary Sumner visualized "A world where God's love is shown through loving, respectful and flourishing relationships". This was not only a hope but a goal actively pursued by praying, campaigning and enabling.

Mothers' Union Vision
A Christ-centered ministry impacting families and communities worldwide.

Mothers' Union Mission
To demonstrate the Christian faith by transforming families and communities in action

Mothers' Union Focus
Promoting stable marriage and family life

Aim of Mothers' Union
The Mothers' Union's aim is to be a transformational and worldwide fellowship bringing Christian care for families of all kinds. This is delivered through our three strategic steps: Pray for relationship to be flourishing and loving; Enable development of all kinds: - Economic, relational and personal so that family life is strengthened; Campaign for social justice for those on the margins and for greater recognition of the value of stable family life.

Mothers' Union Objectives
To uphold Christ;s teaching on the nature of marriage and promote its wider understanding. To encourage parents to bring up their children in the faith and life of the church. To maintain a worldwide fellowship of Christians united in prayer, worship and service. To promote conditions in society favorable to stable family life and the protection of Children. To help those families in adversity.

Mothers' Union Uganda
Mothers' Union was started in Uganda in 1908 by Mrs. Weatherhead, a missionary at Namirembe Diocese in Kampala. Since then Mothers' Union has spread to all the dioceses of the Church of Uganda. In 2008 the Province of the Church of Uganda celebrated 100 years of Mothers Union in Uganda. The Mothers' Union Madi and West Nile Diocese participated fully in the provincial celebrations.

Mothers' Union Madi and West Nile Diocese
In Madi and West Nile Diocese Mothers' Union started in 1989 with the first members commissioned at Ringili Theological College during the regime of Bishop Ephraim Adrale and Canon Salome Adrale. The second group of Mothers Union to be commissioned was from Emmanuel Cathedral and included Rev Canon Rose Adroko, Philister Bileti, Nolah Onzima, Canon Salome Adrale, Jesca Zoodia. From this start in 1989, the Mothers Union membership has kept growing in Madi and West Nile Diocese until now.

In our Diocese, the Mothers' Union is a part of the Missions department. Its activities are coordinated by the Women's Office and led by an Executive headed by a President. Before the start of Mothers' Union, the Women's Office was led by Mary Maclure, an Africa Inland Missionary, and she was succeeded by Rev Canon Penina Enyaru. From 1989 when Mothers' Union was started, Dinah Anefoa Alidri, Canon Salome Adrale, Rev. Canon Sr. Rose Adroko and Rev Canon Alice Bayo and Rev Adiru Victoria Bayo, worked as Mothers' Union workers, coordinating all women's activities in the Diocese: The following were the Presidents of Mothers' Union: Late Canon Salome Adrale, Philister Bileti, Zillah Drati, Canon Sally Anguyo and Hellen Enzama.

The Mothers' Union Membership
Mothers' Union membership is open firstly to those women who have wedded in Church. The second category are widows and single women who are of advanced age (50 years above) whom the Church Council approves and they have stable faith in Christ. The third category is the Associate Members. These are the first wives who are traditionally married and are regular members of the church. It is hoped that they may wed soon. Once they are wedded in the Church, they become full members of Mothers Union. A good number of associates after wedding have become Mothers Union leaders in Archdeaconry and the Cathedral.

Key Activities of Mothers Union
The members have weekly fellowship meetings on Mondays held on a rotational basis i.e. from home to home especially to homes going through difficult times. Members of these homes are encouraged through the word of God and material support. Teaching and training of mothers is provided on various topics such as: the roles of members of Mothers' Union; bringing up children; sanitation and health; household income and supporting husbands; identifying and comforting families in adversity; counseling services to couples, when during weddings some four Mothers' Union and Fathers' Union members join the couple for purposes of counseling; vocational skills imparting particularly tailoring and catering skills for disadvantaged girls; school ministry: e.g. visiting primary, secondary and tertiary institutions and talking to girls sometimes boys too, on selected topics i.e. boy-girl relationship, dressing code, health, HIV/AIDS, afforestation (tree planting) of about 5 acres; Mothers' Union Nursery school set up to earn income for Mothers' Union.

Provision of comfortable accommodation for guests in the "Jehovah Jireh Guest House"
The idea of a guest house came during Canon Salome Adrale's time when she was Mothers' Union worker, but the actual work took off in 2006 when Rev Canon Rose Adroko was the worker and Canon Sally Anguyo was the president.
The Mothers' Union guest house has so far hosted about 1000 guests. Notable high profile guests include: Retired Archbishop Henry Luke Orombi and Phoebe Orombi, Archbishop Stanley Ntagali and Mama Beatrice Ntagali, Hon Lematia Ruth, Former Mothers Union Provincial President Rev Dr Edita Mary Mujinga, Sarah Kasule Provincial Community Development Coordinator, Robert De Berry from Barnabas Fund, Dr William David from Winchester, Brigadier Moses Rwakitarate of Uganda Airforce Headquarters Entebbe, Mrs. Ihla Hooyer and her Family from USA and Bishop Joel Obetia.

These are some of the comments made by guests who have stayed in the Mothers' Union Guest House: "Thank God for his faithfulness. Thank you very much for the great work in the Mothers' Union. Pleasant resting place, clean and quiet. Wonderful place to stay in. Thank you for the reception rendered. God bless you. Thank you for your warm welcome and excellent hospitality."

The money realized from the Guest House has been used to build the perimeter wall, construct more rooms for accommodation in the premises and for the management of the place.

Achievements of Mothers' Union
Since the Mothers' Union was established in Madi and West Nile Diocese, a lot has been achieved. Many women and other Christians have confessed Jesus as Lord and Saviour. Some communities have been impacted, through the work of the Eagle Process, hence using God given resources to change their lives. The number of wedded couples has increased greatly, leading to increase in membership. The number of young wedded wives who have joined Mothers' Union is encouraging especially in the urban area. New infrastructure has been registered, such as the Guest house, Nursery school, the Tailoring school, and Tree Planting. Many churches, parishes and archdeaconries now have guest houses. Muslim evangelism has been developed by supporting Muslim girls who have been disowned by their families because of confessing Jesus Christ as their Saviour.

Challenges Faced by Mothers' Union
We have lost members through death and the majority of members are elderly. Work force becomes difficult, also women at time mistake Mothers' Union to be for elderly women. Many planned activities are not implemented due to limited funds. Many young women fear to join Mothers' Union due to home responsibilities and other responsibilities or duties at work places. Most of the Executive members have responsibilities at work place, hence face difficulties in Mothers' Union work.

8.2 Christian Women Fellowship (CWF)
by Rev Sister Canon Rose Adroko and Canon Margret Ejoga

MOTTO: "ARISE AND SHINE" Isaiah 60:1
What is Christian Women Fellowship?
It is a Christian organization that brings together all Christian women who are baptized, confirmed and communicants. The membership is open to both married and single women. Before a woman is commissioned into CWF, she has to undertake an instructional course which is not less than six months. After the six months she is then inducted into CWF by a clergy.

When was it started?
CWF was conceived in 1904 by a missionary, Venerable Can. George Kryston Baskerville. It was started in Uganda in 1905. The organization in Uganda is now one hundred and thirteen years old. Through Christian Women Fellowship, many people were reached with the Gospel, including people practicing sorcery and witchcraft. Chiefs at all levels are accepted to get married in the church and many became strong supporters of these women. In Uganda, Bishop Ssekadde and Bishop Livingstone Mpalanyi Nkoyoyo and others supported CWF very much.

CWF in West Nile
By 1977, Mrs Mary Maclure, an Africa Inland Missionary, was already working with women in the whole of West Nile Region. Because of her good work she was loved very much. To continue the work she started, she trained Rev. Can. Rose Adroko and Rev. Can. Penina Enyaru Dorish in Women's Ministry; Rev. Can. Rose Adroko, while in Kampala, got the CWF booklet from Namirembe Cathedral. She came to share the content with Bishop Joel Obetia. Bishop Obetia liked the idea of formally establishing the CWF in the diocese. So in 2007, 15 women, at least one from each of the 10 Archdeaconries and the Cathedral were called together for training.

In 2008 the 15 women who were trained were commissioned at Emmanuel Cathedral by Bishop Obetia as the first CWF members. This small beginning of 15 members in 2008 has grown to over 2000 members today in Madi and West Nile Diocese. Some of the first commissioned CWF members are Everline, Yesko, Dinah Angulega, Joyce, Gboya, Suzan, Joyce, Jesca, Margret and Mary Atiku, Prisila, Grace, Mary Letia, Hellen Andreku, Margret Onzima. They formed the Executive Committee of the CWF.

CWF in Madi West Nile was started to encourage people with different gifts to use them to build the church which is the body of Christ (1 Corinthians 12:4 – 30; 1 Corinthians 10:17) Jesus said the harvest is plentiful but the workers are few. CWF encourages young women for the future church to be active in the Church, encouraging the members and preparing them for weddings, which is happening. Many Christian Women Fellowship members are getting wedded to-date.

Each Member of the Christian Women Fellowship has these objectives:
To endeavor to attend church services every Sunday, to pray every day for myself and those people God entrusted to me, to endeavor to attend fellowship meetings, to be obliged to groom children in the Christian belief and discipline, to uplift the welfare of myself and those people entrusted to me spiritually, morally socially and physically, to volunteer in church services, to care for the needy.

Activities in Christian Women Fellowship
Bible study; Educative seminars; Music, Dance and Drama competitions; Weaving e.g Mats, baskets and knitting sweaters; Poultry farming; Subsistence farming; Preaching and teaching

Achievements
We attended Focus Festival Conference once at Lweza in 2010 and we learnt a lot. We gained physically and spiritually so we made it a point to encourage other women to attend every year to date.

We also organized one Focus Festival in our Diocese where we got visitors from Kampala too. Women conferences have been organized by Christian Women Fellowship every year in the Diocese, where the number of women has been growing, and at lower levels too, i.e archdeaconries and parishes. We have organised home visiting and visit to Prisons and Hospitals, the women's fellowship once every week. The church seems more active than before due to involvement of the Christian Women Fellowship, souls have been won for Christ, children have been brought up in the church and there has been an empowerment of women for ministry.

Christian Women Fellowship worked with a number of Bishops and Women Workers.
In 1978 Bishop Remelia Ringtho transferred Rev. Canon Peninah Enyaru from St. Philips Church in Arua Town to work in the Women's Office. While there, she involved women in many activities including making local crafts. When Bishop Remelia was succeeded by Bishop Ephraim Adrale in 1988, he appointed Mrs. Dinnah Alidri as the Women's Worker who was replaced by Mrs. Salome Adrale, the wife of Bishop Adrale. It was also around this time when the Mothers' Union was started in the diocese, so Mrs. Adrale worked as Christian Women and Mothers' Union Worker up to the time of Rt. Rev. Dr Lee Enock Drati.

During Bishop Drati's time, the office of women split into two, i.e Mothers' Union office was under the leadership of Mrs. Salome Adrale, then Christian Women was led by Mrs. Jane Miria. When the time of Mrs. Salome Adrale's retirement came, Rev Can Capt Rose Adroko was transferred to Mothers' Union office as Mothers' Union Worker.

Rev Can Capt Rose Adroko continued to work in the Mothers' Union office up to Bishop Joel Obetia's time in the year 2005. In the Diocesan Synod, Bishop declared that the two women offices were to be merged and be cared for by Rev Can Capt Rose Adroko.

8.3 Madi and West Nile Diocese Fathers' Union
by Canon Joseph Mutebi

Background During a Mothers' Day on June 20, 1909 in Washington DC, Sonora Smart Dodd was struck by the idea of honoring the Fathers too. When Sonora was sixteen, her mother had died giving birth to her sixth child. Sonora reckoned that single parenting was not easy as her father did a wonderful job bringing up the family. She decided that her father's role and the role of fathers worldwide should be recognised should be recognised.

The first Father's Day was observed in Spokane YMCA on the 3rd Sunday of June, 1910 in Washington DC, when attributes of *courage, selfless support, parental sacrifice and of a loving man were celebrated*. In June 1916 President Woodrow Wilson was the first US president to celebrate Father's Day at a party his family hosted. The next President Calvin Coolidge declared it a National holiday in 1924. Johnson Lyndon made Father's Day a holiday to be celebrated on the 3rd Sunday of June, formally agreed by a Congresssional Act in 1972, setting it permanently on the 3rd Sunday in June all over the Nation. Sonora Smart Dodd lived to see her idea come to fruition. She died in 1978 at the ripe old age of 96.

This day became a National Ceremony in many US States and in the Church of England. In countries where the Catholic Church holds greater influence, Father's Day is celebrated on St Joseph's day (March 19). The Anglican Church and other Episcopal Churches worldwide celebrate Fathers' Union Day on St Peter's Day on June 29.

Fathers' Union was founded in Uganda when the Anglican Church of Uganda was still part of the Church of England. Fathers' Union activities started in late 1970's or 1980s. By September 1990 when the constitution was finally approved, the Fathers' Union as a church organisation was well established. It has been growing stronger ever since.

In Madi and West Nile, the organisation started with not so much enthusiasm in 2007. Up until June 2009, Emmanuel Cathedral Mvara had twenty six members who were commissioned in one group. In other Archdeaconries, there were very few members in any one church congregation, but currently there are a total of 504 member in the entire diocese, as shown in the table below:

Archdeaconry	2009	2013	2018
Emmanuel Cathedral	26	39	36
Arua Rural-Jiako			155
Arua Urban			110
Vurra			33
Madi-Oyibu			13
Koboko			55
Maracha			46
Terego			27
Rhino Camp			11
Madi-Moyo			7
Aringa-Yumbe			11
Total			504

Vision: The Vision of the Fathers' Union recognises that: -*"To be undisputedly exemplary Christian fathers who love, worship and serve God"* (Titus 1:6)

Mission: The Mission of the Fathers' Union is: *"To build God Fearing fathers and prosperous Christian families through focussed leadership".* (Proverbs: 22:4, Psalms: 128)

Objectives: The objectives are aimed at promoting Christian living in families without prejudice to the generalities as follows:

To mobilise resources, equip and promote spiritual growth and development.

To empower parents with skills, so as to raise children in a godly manner.

To support initiatives aimed at improving conditions of living for individuals and groups.

To develop special programs to focus on legal and traditional status of families.

Activities: The main activities include:- Organise Bible study sessions, conduct trainings, spiritual retreats, support counselling sessions that enhance family values.

Establish relationships with local and international agencies.

Identify investment opportunities to increase the level of income for the Fathers' Union.

Provide any such lawful and charitable activities.

The **main accomplishments** include:
The overall Diocesan constitution has been instituted to help operate under one umbrella of Madi and West Nile Diocese. Until 2017, the different Archdeaconries operated independently. Annual Work plans are in place to guide operations of the Union. We hold annual St. Peter's Day celebration on June 29 or any close Sunday at congregation level. Fathers' Union instruments of identity such as a flag, anthem and attire have been commissioned.

8.4: Boys' Brigade and Girls' Brigade in the Madi and West Nile Diocese by Rev Grace Bileni and Jacob Angualuga

The Boys' Brigade and the Girls' Brigade are international, interdenominational and uniformed Christian organizations. The Boys' Brigade (BB) was started by a Sunday School Teacher called William Alexander Smith on October 4, 1883 in Glasgow, Scotland. He was knighted in 1908 for his services to youth. Sir William Smith is considered to be a pioneer of Youth Services in UK.

The Girls' Brigade (GB) was formed from the uniting of the Girls' Life Brigade of Ireland (formed in 1893) with the Girls' Guildry of Scotland and the Girls' Life Brigade of England, in 1964.

The first BB Company of Uganda was started by Rev. Canon Orpwood in Kigezi in 1933. The first BB Company in West Nile was started by Rev. Robert N. Booth in Paidha in 1964. The first GB Company in Uganda was started by Miss Christine Walker in West Nile in 1965 at Arua Teacher Training College.

The 5th West Nile BB Company was established in Arua Teacher Training College with the Junior Section in Arua Demonstration School, with Mr. Richard Grinsted as the first Captain. He was followed by Mr. Stewart Cole, Mr. Barnabas Avinyia, Mr. Ronald Buga and Mr. Jacob Angualuga. Venerable Hezekia Ajule served as the Company Chaplain. Mr. Jacob Angualuga became the first Captain of the 5th West Nile Company Junior Section. While Rev. Semi Draku served as the Section's Chaplain.

By 1996 there were 25 registered BB Companies, while the GB registered Companies were over 30. In the diocese by 2018 there are over 100 officers of all ranks and over 300 boys and girls of all ranks. The increased number of the companies and members called for the formation of a Diocesan Council and Archdeaconry Group Councils. The Archdeaconry leaders are called Centre Officers. The following held offices at Diocesan level: The Diocesan Bishop is the Patron for both BB and GB. The following were officers for GB: Queen in 2000 was Mrs. Salome Adrale (Canon), Field Officer was Mrs. Grace Bileni (Rev.) Assistant Field Worker was Mrs. Lois Angualuga, Treasurer was Mrs. Margret Debo. For BB the following held offices: Mr. Barnabas Avinyia was the Patron, Mr. Jacob Angualuga was the Field Officer, while Mr. Tadayo Dema was the Assistant Field Officer, and Mr. Shem Ovua was the Treasurer.

By 2000 the following served as Centre Officers at Archdeaconry levels: For Aringa was Joshua Andruga for BB, for Arua was Richard Omua for BB and for GB was Oripa Agotre; for Arua Urban Wilson Atibuni for BB and for GB was Eunice Ezaru; for Koboko was George Isaac Ombadebo; for Madi was Thomas Makpe Vundru; for Oyibu was Joel Smith Andama for BB and Miriba Mika was for GB; Rhinocamp had Milton Asea; for Maracha was Albert Aziku (Rev.) and Margret Badaru was for GB; for Terego Salimu Jokindu was for BB and Sarah

Maandebo was for GB; Vurra had Tadayo Dema for BB and Jane Dodo was for GB and the Cathedral Mvara had Shem Ovua for BB and Lois Angualuga was for GB.

The above structures have been established to enable BB and GB achieve their objectives which include: To advance Christ's Kingdom among boys and girls there by winning them for Christ; To create healthy behaviour-change among them in respect to social life and interactions; To equip young Christians in techniques of leadership and evangelism; To create National identity among the members; To enrich, enlarge, refresh and enjoy living in new environment with new approaches to life.

These objectives have been derived from the original objective of BB as: "The advancement of Christ's Kingdom among boys and the promotion of habits of Obedience, Reverence, Discipline, Self-respect and all that tends towards a true Christian Manliness." The badge of BB from the beginning is a crest which has an Anchor with the letters BB with words "SURE AND STEDFAST." The motto comes from Hebrews 6:9. The motto for the GB is "SEEK, SERVE AND FOLLOW CHRIST." as found in Matthew 7:7.

The GB and BB members and their banner taking part in the Centenary March from Ezuku to Mvara in February 2018.

The members of BB and GB have been involved in many activities. These include their regular parades, group Bible Studies, playing games and learning new songs. The members actively participate in the following at their churches: lead praises, read lessons, lead prayers and worship, some preach. The members participate in various activities during major diocesan functions and they also render services to the needy. From time to time they are invited to guide people during government functions like independence celebrations. Before a number of brass bands were developed in the region, BB provided a band to lead the march-past during government celebrations.

BB and GB have continued to organize basic and refresher courses for their members at Diocesan and Archdeaconry levels. These courses are on drills, social services, specialized courses such as youth education and development; HIV Aids; Behaviour Change; Health Education; Modern Technology; Cooking and Food Preservation; Discipleship; First Aid and Life-Saving Skills and Leadership Development.

GB and BB Week: these weeks fall in June and July annually for GB and BB respectively. During the week all members are asked to contribute towards the Companies. They go out to friends and the public to ask them to contribute to the GB and BB. The funds collected are shared as follows: 40% to the company the member belongs to, 20% goes to the Diocesan offices and 40% goes to the National Headquarters. All this is done using the slogan, "We want to make our Company BIGGER and BETTER and we want the Brigade in Uganda to be BIGGER and BETTER."

BB and GB Camp Festivals and Competitions: the camps are held rotationally, moving from Archdeaconry to Archdeaconry, and have always been welcomed and supported. They give opportunities for members to get to know each other, work together in order to win in the competitions: Evangelism, set-piece songs in Lugbara and original compositions, memory verses, quiz, art and craft and offertory. Over the years, evangelism, songs and memory verses have been done well, but in quiz, art and craft and offertory, the members fared badly.

Chapter 9
Organisations Supporting the Growth of the Church in West Nile

9.1: The Story of Here is Life by Canon Anyandru Elly Moses, Executive Director

In Communication, we talk about Target Audience. As an organization, Here is Life's target audience is and has been the Aringa people of Yumbe District in North Western Uganda, bordering South Sudan.

How did Here is Life come about? Over 80% of the population of the Aringa people are Muslim and many joined the Army during Idi Amin's rule. This had two impacts. It was during this time the Church saw many, especially young people, join Islam. The Church, after the overthrow of Idi Amin, suffered very much both in exile and after the return from exile.

In numbers and infrastructure the Church in Aringa was brought almost to nothing. The Christians preferred to live in other parts of Uganda, where Christians were welcomed and felt secure. In the minds of some Aringa Christians the question was, "How can the Church in Aringa be helped to be salt and light in that dark part of Uganda?" In early 1980s some efforts were made to form an organization which could help answer this question.

When the Madi and West Nile Diocese leadership at the time was approached with this idea of forming an organization to be working with the Christians in Aringa, they were told that Christian Rural Service (CRS) was enough to work with the Church in Aringa, so there was no need to start another Para-Church Organization. Matters went on becoming worse in the Church in Aringa. The Church lands were being taken away. No Muslims were becoming Christians. Young Christians especially girls were getting married to Muslims, a way of converting them to Islam.

In 1986, Isaac Anguyo then a tutor in Muni Teachers College and Chairman of Scripture Union in West Nile, was invited to a Billy Graham Evangelistic Association Conference in Amsterdam. Isaac went with one question, "How can the church be strengthened to be able to reach Muslims for Christ?" Indeed at this conference, Anguyo found many Christian organizations working to reach Muslims for Christ and empowering the Christians to do so and disciple their own people.

When Anguyo came back, in his own words, "I lost interest in teaching and desired to see some work done in Aringa." He approached Samson Waiga, who was working in Uganda Commercial Bank in Arua, and Hampton Alokore, a school teacher in Arua, to share his burden for the Aringa. The two Aringa became excited and now, with Anguyo, these three looked for ways of reaching the Aringa for Christ.

They thought if they started an organization bringing the Aringa in Arua together, this would give them the opportunity to share Jesus Christ's love with the Muslims, beginning from Arua. When they shared their desire to bring the Aringa together, the Muslims who became the majority in the organization were very happy and Aringa Development Association (ADA) was formed with Abasi Abua Cucu being the Chairman. In the Executive were Waiga and Alokore.

When Lt. Col John Onaah returned from exile in 1986, our desire to share the Gospel with Muslims and the formation of Aringa Development Association was shared with him. He was not excited and told the three, "How do you hope to reach the Muslims for Christ, when they are in the leadership of the organization. You will not succeed. The organization will just be a social organization which will be dominated by the Muslims."

At the same time, in Aringa County, the Muslims formed Aringa Muslim Development Programme (AMDP) especially in getting the assets Lutheran World Federation (LWF) was giving out after resettling the refugees returning from Sudan. The Aringa Muslims in Arua who were members of ADA, told us, they did not need ADA because their own organization was already formed in Aringa County. So ADA was left to die and efforts to develop a Christian Organization took root.

Anguyo did not have formal training in Bible nor theology. He was admitted to Daystar University College for Bachelor in Liberal Arts (Communication and Community Development and minor courses in theology and Bible). The members at this time were four: Lt. Col. John Dan Onaah, Sam Waiga, Hampton Alokore and Isaac Anguyo. Onaah, Waiga and Alokore were to work to register the organization with the Uganda Government while Anguyo was to share the vision and look for partners. This was at an opportune time as Anguyo was in Nairobi. He had the opportunity to meet and share the vision with many. The courses also enabled him to develop a relevant name. HERE IS LIFE: Jesus said, I am the way, the truth and the life" and "I came that they may have life and have it to the full." So when we are introducing people to Jesus, we are introducing them to LIFE. That was how the name HERE IS LIFE came about. It was also a neutral name.

In 1988 Here is Life was registered as a Company Limited by Shares. At the time it was not easy to register an organization as an NGO. The Four became the first share-holders. Other members were recruited in the organization. Their aim was to empower the Christians in Aringa, Spiritually, Socially and Physically, so that they can share the love of Jesus Christ with many. Indeed activities were planned to help the members achieve these objectives. They got partners to support Here is Life financially and with manpower both locally and internationally.

In 1990, the members asked Isaac Anguyo to be the first Managing Director of Here is Life. Without office space anywhere, Anguyo asked his wife to allow him to occupy the grass thatched guest house sitting room and it became the office of the organization. This was occupied until 1998, when with help of DIGUNA, Here is Life established a radio station. There was a need to move from home room office to Arua Town where we got a rented room for office for the radio. When Voice Of Life 100.9 FM radio station was built on Arua Hill, there was now enough office space. From a rented room Here is Life moved to its offices in 2000.

Over time, Here is Life developed its Mission, Vision and Values as:
The vision of Here Is Life is seeing many people believing in Jesus Christ, growing in their faith and meeting their needs holistically.

The Mission of HIL is enhancing the potentials of a person to enable him or her to live a whole and integrated life that he or she has been created for, through: health, radio, educational programmes; economic activities; creating jobs and providing social services.

The following are **the values** which Here is Life and its members uphold: Moral uprightness, Faithfulness in Jesus Christ and use of resources, Transparency, Honesty, Concern for human life, Respect, Excellence in any undertaking and Sacrifice.

Thematic Areas: Here Is Life operates using the following thematic areas to reach its goal**:** Community empowerment for socio economic development; Community education through FM radio programs; Peace building among communities; Emergency Disaster response natural and man-made like refugees**;** Literacy and translation of materials into Aringa language; Water Sanitation and Hygiene (WASH) among refugees and host community; Leadership development; Livelihood vocational skills development in carpentry and joinery, tailoring, Agriculture and business development skills and Advocacy.

The Achievements ofHere is Life:
Thirty years along the way, Here is Life has achieved much. Lives of people in Aringa have changed, Christ has been witnessed to, and some Muslims have believed in Christ, some who have been persecuted have been looked after by some Christians.

This is what David Bebb, an internee from Wheaton College USA in 2002 said, "The projects have been successful in making life easier for the Aringas. Women in particular, save much time in grinding of their grain, energy that they can now use and enjoy elsewhere. The stores, likewise, have made life easier by giving Aringas a useful place for selling their grain when it is plentiful and buying more when it is scarce. The employees are witnesses of Christ. I have been blessed in my interactions with the employees of the projects. If they strive to act towards their customers as they have toward me, these five projects can continue to give testimony of Christ to the people of Aringa."

The projects referred to by Bebb were two grain stores, two grinding mills and rice hulling, buying and selling. Although they are no longer functional, they made a lot of impact. What happened to them is another story.

It may help the reader to know what Here is Life has achieved in the 30 years period:

In Economic (Businesses) area the following were achieved:
Two **grinding mills** were established with grants from Tearfund England. With the aim of helping the members get income and lessen the burden on women in domestic work.
Two **food stores** to buy food produce with support from Kinder Not Hilfe. The purpose was to buy food items during harvest and sell them for profit during off-season from February to June.
A community **rice project** for buying rice, hulling and selling for profit was established with support from Tearfund UK. The members also provided hulling services at a cost for customers and encouraged more growing of rice in the community.
With training and financial support from Glory Bee Foods in USA, a h**oney business** under the name **Blessed be For Life Trade Post** was established. The business is owned and managed by Canon Mophart Maffu. The business is providing market, employment and honey as food and medicine to not only Yumbe, but far and wide. Some bee keepers in Yumbe and Koboko Districts sell

their honey to Blessed Bee For Life. Many, including people far from Yumbe, have received training in bee keeping.

Women's project, Samaritan Enterprises, was established as a business and Bible Study Group in Arua Town. The members have supported each other in happy and difficult times.

The Social activities and projects established have impacted many lives.
A vocational school called Evangelical School of Technology in Aringa (ESTA) was established. It had been recruiting Primary 7-S4 leavers to learn skills which help them earn a living. This was becoming a very popular learning centre. Due to both internal and external factors, ESTA is no longer functioning as it was meant to.

A Community Library Service in Yumbe District was established. The library system has over 6,000 books, with a Central Library based at Eleke and six Library Centres scattered within Yumbe District.

Here Is Life helped the Church and community at Rodo in Kei Sub-county to establish a Grade III Health Centre providing in-patient and out-patient services, PHC and HIV/AIDS programmes. The Church and community are supported by the local government and Madi and West Nile Diocesan Health Department.

With support from DIGUNA, a German organization, Here is Life runs an **FM radio station called Voice of Life FM100.9,** stationed on Arua Hill in Arua Town. Voice of Life radio, since November 1997, is reaching people in West Nile Region and surrounding areas including Amuru District, Eastern DR Congo and Southern South Sudan with community empowerment programs like education, entertainment and Christian programs.

Here Is Life developed Aringa language orthography and literacy materials in the language. This was launched in October 2011 by National Curriculum Development Centre. The orthography has given Aringa language the power to be a language written and used in thematic teaching in lower primary schools.

With technical and financial support from SIL and One Book, Here Is life translated the New Testament into Aringa language and the Aringa Christians have the New Testament in their own language. This was launched in a colourful ceremony in 2014.

The New Testament has been recorded into audio with the help of Faith Comes By Hearing (FCBH). The New Testament audio now helps the illiterate and blind to hear the Gospel in Aringa.

In almost every two years Aringa County, now Yumbe, goes into famine. In 2007 HIL provided relief food and seeds to people whose crops were destroyed by too much sun shine and much rain.

After two years in 2009, during another famine which was worse than the 2007 famine, Here is Life provided food aid to the hungry, and supported Yumbe Hospital with food for the feeding centre to feed the malnourished children admitted in the hospital. To meet the food crises of 2011, Here Is Life received shillings 280,000,000 from Barnabas Fund UK and other partners in USA and Germany to provide food aid for 3,500 people, including 50 malnourished children in Yumbe Hospital feeding centre over a period of three months.

Under holistic transformation community empowerment through Participatory Evaluation Process (PEP) and Church and Community Mobilization Process (CCMP), programmes are ongoing in Yumbe, Moyo, Obongi and Adjumani among the nationals.

With technical support from Timothy Training Institute and financial support from Myrtle Grove Evangelical Presbyterian Church, HIL developed Discipleship Work Books for the Church in Yumbe. The series entitled Growing in Grace, has four books: Knowing God, Loving God, Trusting God and Serving God.

With the sudden influx of refugees from South Sudan, with support from World Renew, Here is Life got involved in Emergency Refugee Response in Yumbe District from August 2016 with the programme called Water, Sanitation and Hygiene (WASH), particularly communal latrines for refugees and household latrines for persons with special needs for refugees and the host community, distribution of cleaning kits for latrines and hygiene promotion education.

With funding from Tearfund UK since 2014 Here is Life has been involved in Peace Building and Trauma Healing programmes among refugees from South Sudan. In Adjumani Here is Life is working in the following settlements: Mireyi, Boroli, Pagirinya and Alere. While in Bidi Bidi, it is in Zone 3 refugee settlements in Yumbe Distirct.

Here is Life, like any other human organization, has had a good number of challenges. The first was in its early formative years, well-placed Christians wrote to Aringa Christians in Kampala that Anguyo had brought a religion called Here is Life. They, as members of the Revival, will fight to remove this confusion in Aringa.

The second major challenge was when some Christians went to tell Muslims in Arua Town that Anguyo had got a lot of dollars from USA to convert Muslims into Christianity. These Muslims told Anguyo that they knew what he was doing. He should not worry but go ahead with his work.

The biggest challenges were in 2002 when Reid and Erik were wounded by some gunmen we thought were robbers. Though the lives of these two American missionaries were saved, it somehow scared would-be missionaries to Aringa. The challenge Here is Life has never recovered from is the killing of Warren and Donna Pet, Africa Inland Missionaries from USA, in 2004. These were very brutal killings. Nobody claimed responsibility nor were there arrests leading to prosecutions. To date, Here is Life does not know why these missionaries and a student called Isaac were killed at ESTA.

Here is Life right from the beginning stated that, in Aringa HIL will wish to work with the Church not through the Church. Along the way the local and worldwide church has continued to work with Here is Life. The following organisations, with many individuals, have helped Here is Life reach where it is in 2018, celebrating the Centenary of the Anglican Church in West Nile: Church of Uganda Madi and West Nile Diocese, Tearfund UK, Barnabas Fund UK, Africa Inland Mission, the Evangelical Church in Nazenburg, Germany, Help for Brethren International Germany, Christian Services International Germany, Elmbroke Church USA, Author De'moss Foundation USA, Myrtle Grove Evangelical Presbyterian Church USA, First Presbyterian Church Ipswich USA, World Renew (Formerly CRWRC), Hosanna (Faith Comes By Hearing USA), Timothy Training Institute, Open Doors Kenya, SIL Uganda/Tanzania and OneBook.

When Canon Isaac Jaffer Anguyo felt that there was need to hand over the leadership of Here is Life to a younger person, the process of getting such a person was a challenge. God in His sovereignty saw it fit that in August 2015, he handed over the leadership of Here is Life to Canon Anyandru Elly Moses.

By what is happening in Here is Life as this small history is being written one would say, Canon Isaac Jaffer Anguyo was called 30 years ago by God to lead the church to witness for Christ among the Muslims of Aringa. May the same be said of Canon Anyandru Elly Moses after 30 years.

9.2: Scripture Union in partnership with the Church
by Joshua Anguyo and Canon John Ondoma

Scripture Union was started in UK in 1867 through two Payson Hammond, a controversial American preacher, and Josiah Spiers who had had started the Children Special Service Mission (CSSM). In that Victorian era, the emphasis in the church was to separate children from adults in worship because they would disturb the adults. Hammond and Spiers adopted a new dynamic way of reaching with an emphasis on God's love and on reaching the hearts of young people through songs and hymns that children could easily sing. They started camps at beach sites that encouraged young people to read the Bible and they conducted children services that involved also counseling sessions and keeping contact with the young people by writing letters.

This form of ministry required an interdenominational approach. It was adopted internationally and to date, Scripture Union hasn expanded to over 130 countries worldwide (including Uganda). Their global aims are to work with Churches in mainly two areas, evangelism and discipleship, emphasizing prayer and personal reading of the Bible. Christian growth into maturity through these activities should reflect Jesus and cause a transformation in individuals, families, societies and the nation.

In Uganda, Scripture Union was introduced by missionaries in 1950s to encourage men and women to know God better. Active SU Programmes in Ugandan schools was started by Albert Tailor, a teacher in Mwiri College. In 1963 he resigned from teaching and became the first SU Uganda Staff member. Scripture Union was extended to West Nile, starting with the printing of SU Lugbarati Bible Reading calendars in 1959. These were produced and distributed by SU international office as a nurture programme for discipleship. Later, they were widely used for daily Bible reading by Christians in Madi and West Nile Diocese. Each believer registered and signed for these cards as a form of holding them accountable.

The main focus of Scripture Union by then was evangelism and discipleship by forming Bible based discipleship clubs in schools/institutions, Life skills education/training programme, tailored towards HIV and AIDS prevention among young Christians, positive parenting program which targeted families with Christian values of raising children in the fear of the Lord and encouraging families to relate in love, production and distribution of Bible reading materials and scripture reading guidelines that aimed at grounding and empowering the Christians with truth from the Holy Scriptures.

Scripture Union North-western Region stands on the shoulders of great men and women of God who have remained strong in serving the Lord to date. It is also very clear that their courage and faithful confidence is drawn from the mentorship experiences of the renowned spiritual legacy of key leaders nurtured through Scripture Union. The example of key leaders is a great source of inspiration to the young generation of Scripture Union North Western region, especially: the Rev. Silvanus Wani (the first Archbishop from West Nile), Rt Rev. Ephraim Adrale, Rev. Can. Lusania Kasamba, retired Archbishop of Uganda Henry Luke Orombi, Bishop Joel Obetia, Canon John Ondoma, Kezzy Ondoma, Canon Anguyo Isaac, Solomon Okecha, Rev. Canon Stephen Gelenga, Isaac Drazu, Late Crispo Ozelle, Dr. Lulua Johnson, Barnabas Avinyia and Matua Eliakim. Some of the women role models include: Jane Dodo, Jocelyn Josoru, Joyce Eceru, Joyce Kule Yikiru, Betty Alioru, among others. These men and women have all been members of Scripture Union.

Scripture Union has continued to shape great leaders of moral integrity and character in the West Nile region. We pray to God that Scripture Union will remain a profound and inspiring Christian body that will successively direct the destiny of the young. As Biblical instructions are passed on from generation to generation, life changing values, transformational teachings, deliverance and healing experiences should all result in repentance, forgiveness and salvation in our Lord Jesus Christ across the region and beyond.

School ministry
Scripture Union and the Church have complementing roles in extending the Kingdom of God. This is simply because during the School times, the children and youth are in School. While at School, Scripture Union provides an enabling environment for discipleship and engages the young people to know God and live their lives as faithful Christians. This is carried out through a number of discipleship programmes including establishment of discipleship clubs in Schools, Bible study in groups, Bible stories in plays, leadership development programmes and other activities for proper functioning of the clubs.

On the other hand, the young people during holidays are involved in the local Churches. This perfectly bridges any gaps and provides a great opportunity to continuously engage the young people to keep focus in practicing their Christian faith. It was through this approach that the young people in Scripture Union clubs began to transfer what they learnt from Scripture Union clubs and use the approaches for youth ministry in the Churches which gradually led to the starting of youth services across the Diocese.

Among the first education institutions that started Scripture Union clubs were Mvara SS and Arua Teachers College, Ombatini SS, Uringi SS. It was during these clubs that many leaders today came to know Jesus Christ as their Lord and Saviour. A typical example is the retired Archbishop of Church of Uganda, Rt Rev Henry Luke Orombi. Many missionaries that came to the Diocese including Seaton Marclure, Simon Martin and John Haden have taken part in School ministry and supported Scripture Union activities in the region, physically participated in the activities.

Camps and conferences
Scripture Union Uganda held national conferences in Gayaza, Mwiri, Nabumali and Budo, but these had little involvement of people from up country apart from a few leaders. Having attended and seen the impact of these conferences, our own young men, by then including Can. John Ondoma, Dr. Lulua Johnson, Ismail Obima were provoked to organize conferences themselves with the support of the Madi and West Nile Diocese under the leadership of Rt Rev. Remelia Ringtho. This led to the ever first Scripture Union conference in West Nile in 1976. Since then, conferences expanded as a key activity for starting holidays across the entire region. Through these conferences, leaders were mentored and opportunities were given to young people to accept Jesus as Lord and Saviour. Conferences and camps became widely adopted by the Church as a way of engaging the young people to know God better. The initial conferences of Scripture Union were supported by Madi West Nile Diocese under the leadership of Rt Rev. Remelia Ringtho. We have every reason to thank God for the strong

partnership that has existed between Scripture Union and Madi and West Nile Diocese.

9.3: The Impact Of The Fellowship of Christian Unions (FOCUS) Uganda on the Church in West Nile by Samuel Baker Okullo (Training Secretary, FOCUS West Nile Region, 2008-2013)

Jesus, in Mathew 28:16-20 left the great commission to His disciples and believers *"Therefore, go and make disciples of all nations,"* This too is our mandate as the Church of Christ today of which FOCUS Uganda for the last forty five years has been part of the fulfilment among students in the universities and colleges across Uganda.

FOCUS Uganda was born in the wave of independence from colonial rule in Uganda in 1962 which motivated the formation of the Christian Union at Makerere University. Christianity was taking another dimension of freedom from the missionary churches which were associated with colonialism. From the Christian Union at Makerere University, Kampala, associate groups started meeting in Kampala for Bible Studies which later gave birth to the Fellowship of Christian Unions (FOCUS) Uganda in 1972. FOCUS, a Christian student movement was committed to sharing the good news of Jesus Christ in the universities and colleges, and to nurturing its members into effective witnesses of Christ on campus and in society.

In West Nile region, FOCUS was started through the regional associate groups led by the associate volunteers. Later, through the national FOCUS structure, we appointed a regional training secretary, supported by the regional working committee and the regional associates.

FOCUS ministry has served the Church by sharing the gospel of Jesus Christ within the colleges and universities in West Nile, to bring students to the knowledge of Christ. Campus Students believe in the power to transform the whole world in fulfilment of Acts 1:8 in their time while they are at campus.

Soul winning has become the central belief and practice among Christian students at campuses. The ministry of FOCUS through the various campus mission opportunities i.e. door to door, open air preaching, mission week and peer apologetics, has enabled students to believe that Christians must and are able to engage in any form of evangelistic activities all the time. Due to this radical Christian witnessing, we have seen Christ being preached as students reach out to fellow students, resulting in an increase in the number of believers of Christ in the Church.

Christianity in Africa has received a worldwide reputation as far as numerical growth is concerned. The greatest percentage of Christianity being practiced in Africa is active among students and youth who are radical and energetic. In addition, *"for decades the image the world has had for African Christianity is that of a fat baby, growing fatter every day but never growing up! A baby forever on milk, not on solid food, which is prepared in Africa and fit for international consumption"* (Yemi Ladipo, AJET 1989).

The spiritual depth and commitment on the part of the believers is still wanting and this is because of lack of church emphasis on discipleship. FOCUS Uganda has been standing in this gap by making disciples of Christ among the university and college students for the Church. These has been possible through the various FOCUS discipleship programs like Annual regional students' conference, small group Bible Studies, Care group meetings and discipleship training. The cream of these has been the annual regional students' conference which has seen thousands of students being nurtured and discipled annually. Solomon Nyakuni (from Arua), a former student of Arua School of Nursing had this to say about FOCUS discipleship:

"The discipleship programs of FOCUS helped in modelling and discipling me into what I am today; my eyes have been opened to see Christianity from the Biblical and missional perspective rather than my earlier religious world view."

Developing leaders for Christian service in the Church.

FOCUS ministry has developed servant leaders who are deeply rooted in Christ through the on-campus weekly mentorship from the FOCUS team, semester leadership trainings and annual leadership summit. The ministry of FOCUS in West Nile has developed on average 30 leaders annually in each Christian Union in West Nile (Regional ministry reports). Most of these leaders have had the opportunity to serve in the Christian Union leadership. This enabled them to discover their leadership passion and gifts which has been a blessing to both the service of the local church and the market place ministries. Arike James (from Koboko) the current Training Secretary of FOCUS West Nile Region has this to say about how FOCUS has developed him as a leader:

"When I was completing from campus, I felt prepared and equipped in servant leadership through the mentorship of FOCUS staff and the leadership experience I had as a Christian Union leader at Uganda College of Commerce (UCC) Pakwach. These gave me the confidence to serve as the regional FOCUS leader and providing leadership at my home Church as well."

The ministry of FOCUS has played a big role in developing mission minded Christians for the Church with its missions teaching and trainings. These have remained a great mobilization tool in the Church for global mission. Christian unions across the country have had a tradition of one week-end seminar missions to the communities in need of the Gospel of Jesus Christ. This presented opportunities for the young men and women who are energetic and growing in Christ to discover and practice their mission passion.

We have seen many rural places and needy communities like Adjumani, Moyo, Yumbe in West Nile being reached by the Christian Union students for Jesus in partnership with the local churches. Such missions have so far witnessed overwhelming miracles of salvations, healing and deliverance accompanied by social action of helping the poor and the needy. As the students respond to this call to missions, the mandate of the local church is being fulfilled. Youth in those mission fields are encouraged and motivated to be involved practically in the mission of the Church

The ministry of FOCUS Uganda has provided pastoral care for the students in the colleges and universities in partnership with the Chaplaincy Departments. The staff and associates of FOCUS Uganda have always had a passion to go back to the Christian unions and the chaplaincy to support the needy students through pastoral care. It's important to note that, most of the university and college students come at the age of critical decision making which has life implication for their future.

Most of them would be struggling with issues of love relationship, career, family challenges and even how to grow in the fear of the Lord as a young man or woman. The staff and associates of FOCUS Uganda have been playing the critical role of an uncle or auntie to the Christian union and chapel students by sharing their life experience with them, opening their homes to host them, mentoring in family life and any form of pastoral care support a young man or woman would desire in his or her Christian life as a student.

The church in Uganda has been on the receiving end of global mission as the mission field for years and yet the current statistics according to the Ugandan Census, 2014 indicates that Christianity in Uganda stands at 84.5% of the total population of Uganda. The core question for the church now is *"How can the Ugandan Church move from the being the mission field to the mission force?"*

As the Church in West Nile celebrates her centenary of Christianity, let's reflect and seek the face of God on how we can attract and translate the passionate, energetic and gifted workforce we have at the various universities and colleges through FOCUS Uganda, to serve as the feet that would take the gospel, the knees that would pray for global mission and the hand that would give towards the global mission in a bid to make Uganda a mission force.

9.4: The Bible translations by Asiku Gift Olema and Canon Barnabas Delu
The 1966 Wild Fire!
The reason why the Bible is very important is because it is God's word and it transforms lives. This centenary is a time we can remember the journey of Bible translation into Lugbarati and other languages in West Nile. More so, in a special way we will commend mission organisations, individual missionaries, native speakers, the church and community at large for their tremendous contribution to bringing God's word to the heart of the Lugbara.

"Bible translation into Lugbarati has made God to fit in the culture of the Lugbara." Bishop Joel Obetia, 2009.

When the Lugbara Bible arrived to the enthusiastic and expectant Lugbara speakers in West Nile in 1966, there was an explosion of Christianity in the region. The Wild Fire ignited by the Good News in the heart language of the region still burns brightly today. Several new church congregations were formed, the Madi and West Nile Diocese which was formed earlier is maturing, the doors were opened for more missionaries to come in addition to those from AIM and CMS.

The Roman Catholic Church fully moved into West Nile bringing new missions to Arua Archdiocese (Arua Diocese). Primary and Secondary Schools were established, hospitals were built and run by the Church to meet the physical needs of the community. The Church did what Jesus did, feed the hungry, heal the sick, forgive the accused and encourage repentance. There was an immediate impact, which showed that God's word is powerful because it transforms life.

The impact and power of God's word in the mother tongue was immediate, breaking through into the West Nile region, which is probably more linguistically diverse than any other region in Uganda. It is home to several language families not found anywhere else in Uganda or East Africa. These include: Lugbara, Ma'di, Kebu, Bari, Luluba or Mangbetu, which belong to the Central Sudanic family; Gungu, which is Bantu; Nubi, which is an Arabic based Creole; Kakwa, which is Eastern Nilotic; and Alur, which is Western Nilotic. In essence, all the language families in Uganda are present today in this region.

In this article we want to recognise and honour the Arua Catholic Diocese for immediately taking on the mantle to translate the Bible into Lugbara. This drive increased the impact of God's word in the region and hugely contributed to the Christian revolution in the 20th Century. Various lectionaries were prepared by the Catholics from 1926, the Matthew and Mark diglots in Lugbara and English were published in 1960 and 1964 respectively by Kisubi Marianum Press and Psalms translated by Frs. John Ferrazin and Antony Androa, published in 1979 in Vicenza, Italy.

The West Nile Christian revolution crossed the borders to Zaire (Congo) and Sudan. Thousands of copies of the Lugbara Bible were distributed across the border and both native and non-native Lugbara speakers were determined to own a copy and learn to read God's word in Lugbarati.

It is right to say that 1966 was the year when the West Nile region received language independence to communicate to God in the language of the heart of the people, four years after Uganda's Independence in 1962 from the British Protectorate Government. The Lugbara Bible was finally published and distributed in the West Nile Districts. They were set on fire for evangelism and mission. The Anglican Church exploded with multiple new congregations, sending people from West Nile as missionaries to other regions (like Northern Uganda, Eastern Congo, and Sudan), the East African Revival movement's roots deepened and Lugbara became a language for the people to communicate directly with Almighty God.

The same power of God's word can be seen today. Wherever the Lugbara live in any part of Uganda, they will congregate and form a Church or hold a service in Lugbarati. For example, Okuvu Church in Kampala, St. Francis Chapel in Makerere, Kampala, St. John's Church in Entebbe and many other congregations across Uganda.

In this centenary celebration, we thank God for his World Wide Church of Christ which fully supported the work, the AIM and CMS missionaries, the Bible Society of East Africa, Bible Society of Uganda, the West Nile local church, the Roman Catholic Church for the various lectionaries started in 1926 and individuals mentioned in this chapter.

Why was the Bible translated?

Biscuit-tin Bible-1896

In 1896, the Luganda Bible was the first to appear in any of the languages in Uganda and the second in East and Central Africa after Kiunguja Swahili Bible. The 1896 Luganda Bible translation was popularly known as the "Biscuit-tin Bible". This was probably because it was the size of the tin boxes used by Baganda to store biscuits and other valuables and books.

The Luganda Bible was pioneered by CMS missionaries Alexander Morehead Mackay, Robert Pickering Ashe and Edward Cyril Gordon, and it was the work of translators George Lawrence Pilkington, Henry Wright Dita Kitaakule, Samwili Mukasa among others.

In 1890, George Lawrence Pilkington arrived in Uganda after receiving his call to mission. With his charismatic outlook to missions, he became a leader in the

Christian revival which swept Buganda starting from 1893-1894. He was instrumental in spearheading this revival which later gave birth to the **Tukutendereza** revival movement. A wild fire spread across the country reaching the West Nile region with power.

Translation of the Bible into Lugbara
The people of the Amazon region asked the missionary Cameron Townsend:
"If your God is powerful, why can't He speak my language?"

The people of West Nile asked the same question. Putting this question into context, the "Mundu" was not able to speak Lugbarati. He knew Swahili and Luganda, hence the 1896 translated Bibles. To the native Lugbara, God came on Sunday's and went away for a full week and then returned the next Sunday. He was not the God of the Lugbara without the Lugbara Bible. For the people of West Nile, God was a foreigner just like the AIM and CMS missionary "Mundu" who brought the Good News.

Preaching the Good News in Luganda or Swahili in the West Nile region landed in shallow waters and the English Bible was not any better. The best language God could speak to his people in the West Nile was and is Lugbarati which was already popular in the region. Christianity in the West Nile region could only be effective, deeply and widely accepted in the local language, Lugbarati, alongside other languages and dialects already spoken in the region.

During the early stages of translation of the Bible into Lugbara, the Central Sudanic language family in West Nile was grouped into two: High Lugbara from Terego going down to Logiri and Ma'di Okollo, and Low Lugbara, this was Aringa. The Lugbara Bible translation work pioneered by AIM was mainly in the High Lugbara. Aringa was considered to be at 71% mutual intelligibility with high Lugbara. But according to a survey done by Summer Institute of Linguistics (SIL) in 1995-1998, it was discovered that Aringa is 75% different from High Lugbara, which then qualified Aringa for language development and a Bible translation of its own.

Several missionaries enabled the translation of the Bible into Lugbara:
- Rev. C. H. Mount was the first to attempt translation into Lugbara of the Gospel of Mark published by the BFBS in 1922.
- The Gospel of Luke was translated by Agnes H. Bell of the AIM and published by British Foreign Bible Society (BFBS) in 1926, and in the same year the Gospel and Epistle of John was translated by J.W. Bell and A.H. Bell, while the Epistle of James was translated by Kate Mather, all published by BFBS London in 1926.

Others books or portions translated into Lugbara include

Book	Translated by	Publisher	Year
Matthew	Rev. G. Fred B. Morris	BFBS	1928
Acts	A.E. Vollor	BFBS	1928
Romans, 1 &2 Peter, Corinthians	A.E Vollor	BFBS	1929
Galatians, Thessalonians	A.E. Vollor	BFBS	1933
Mark *(revised)*	A.E. Vollor	BFBS	1933
Romans *(revised)*	Laura I. Barr	BFBS	1952

We can confidently assert that the responsibility for finalising the translation and revision of the New Testament into Lugbara was borne by A. E. Vollor, Florence M. Vollor, Hellen Nothing and Anne Souther and it was published in 1936. Rev. A.E. Vollor wanted to translate the entire Lugbara Bible and continued with translating some Old Testament books (Pentateuch). However, his vision for the Lugbara Bible faced a strong challenge from the Government education policy which demanded the use of Swahili for teaching across East Africa.

Although Rev. A.E. Vollor put forward a strong case for translating the Bible into Lugbara before BFBS representatives in London, he lost his case due to the Government education policy supporting Swahili. However, God's will prevailed over the judgement of BFBS and Rev. A.E. Vollor's mantle was fully picked up by Rev. A. Seton Maclure and Miss Laura Belle Barr (AIM), who were assisted by an African translation checking committee. The team locally printed several single Old Testament books as they promoted literacy in Lugbarati.

In 1949 the Lugbara Language Committee adopted a new orthography recommended by Dr. A. N. Tucker of London. This then led to the revision of the 1936 New Testament by Miss Laura Belle Barr with the assistance of Canon A. S. Maclure and a committee. The following people were in the team which greatly contributed towards the revision of the New Testament: Mary and Seton Maclure, Laura Belle Barr assisted by H.T. Ajule, Benon Obetia, N. Yii, Y. Debo, N. Foro, K. Angondubo, M. Andama and Baritolomayo Godo. The revised Lugbara New Testament was published in 1960.

October 1960 was a breakthrough for Canon. A. Seton Maclure when he was able to report from Arua, Uganda to the BFBS, London that,

> "....the basic work on the translation of the Old Testament and revision of the New Testament was completed. Work is beginning on the preparation of references."

In 1964, the relevant BFBS committee

> "Resolved to recommend that the text of the Bible in Lugbara be accepted as conforming to the rules for Translators" and therefore met the condition for publication by BFBS.

1966 was the year of triumph when the labours of A. E. Vollor, Laura Belle Barr, H.T. Ajule, B. Obetia, N. Yii, Y. Debo, N. Foro, and others on the translation committee culminated in the first complete Lugbara Bible, published by Bible Society of East Africa, Nairobi.

Other publications:
It was not only Scriptures which were translated. The Lugbara Hymn and Prayer Book was immediately published. These added to the revival in the region. The

people were now able to sing hymns and read God's word in the language they use every day for good and bad things for example, blessing and cursing, encouraging and discouraging, rebuking and rewarding, worshipping God and visiting witch doctors and others. In addition, several educational and health materials were produced in Lugbara by the Church and government for schools, hospitals and agricultural purposes.

The Aringa Translation

The most recent milestone was 24th June 2014 when the Aringa New Testament was launched in Yumbe. All religions in the region fully participated in the launch. Christians purchased copies of the New Testament for Muslims while the Muslims did the same for Christians. The reason why God's word is important in our mother tongue is because it is very powerful and it is the only book that can transform lives with immediate impact. Aringa Bible translation has come a long way and there is still work in progress with Old Testament translation.

Reading Aringa NT together

1988 was the year of massive evangelism by the Madi and West Nile Diocese in partnership with DIGUNA a German Christian organisation. They came to serve in Aringa County which brought a breakthrough and an increased desire for God's word in Aringa. The population of Aringa constitutes 10% Christian while the other 90% are either Muslem or practice African Traditional Religion or do not have any faith affiliation. The Uganda 2014 census report puts the Aringa population at 587,000 people across the Country.

God raised faithful men among the Aringa to bring the Good News to Aringa people in their own language. This desire for mission and ministry led to the formation and registration of "Here is Life" (HIL) in 1988 under the faithful leadership of Canon Isaac Anguyo, who championed the vision to translate the New Testament into Aringa. When Summer Institute of Linguistics-Sudan branch (SIL International) moved to Uganda to establish their offices in Arua, HIL leadership took the initiative to approach SIL to help with developing the language and to help with Bible translation in 1998.

SIL (Sudan Branch) started the process to work with HIL in 1998. Later, SIL-UTB (Uganda Tanzania Branch) supported the project from 2006 to date. A survey to determine whether Aringa is a language different enough for translation was done from 1995 to 1998. Aringa is discovered to be 75% different from Lugbara (High-Lugbara). So SIL agreed to assist the language development. The team started the work of translation with the book of Genesis in 1999, which was completed in 2000. The New Testament work started in 2001 and it took 13 years to translate the Aringa New Testament, which was launched 3 years later on 24th June 2016. The Old Testament work started in 2015 and will continue until it is finished.

Sincere thanks go to SIL International for partnering with HIL in giving technical support for the translation, to OneBook for funding, to the Bible Society of Uganda for distribution, to the Church in Uganda and Madi and West Nile Diocese for all the support which brought to fruition the Aringa New Testament.

We are so grateful to God for enabling the following translators to start and finish translation of Aringa New Testament and ensure that it was printed and distributed in their life time. The translators included, Canon Banabas Delu, James Ezaruku, Andrew Angupale while Alex Angoli and Unduga Charles worked on the side of Literacy and Scripture Engagement. The team was led by Canon Isaac Anguyo who motivated, influenced, encouraged and linked the project to other partners. God is indeed gracious.

The translation team had a strong pillar, the community; Christians and Muslims all came together for the sake of their language and made useful contributions which led to the good quality translation of the Aringa New Testament. It is an accurate, clear, natural and fluent translation based on a carefully researched and developed orthography. We acknowledge the significant contribution of John and Joy Anderson, John Macaulay, Waller Tabb, Enoch Wandera and other SIL staff who served as Consultants for this translation.

Other languages in West Nile with a complete Bible or Portions

No	Language	1st Portion/Book	1st NT	1st Bible
1	Alur	1921	1933	1936
2	Lugbara	1922	1936	1966
3	Kakwa	1967	1974	1983
4	Ma'di (Moyo)	1935	1977	
5	Kebu	1964	1995	1995
6	Aringa	2000	2014	
7	Ndrulo *(Lendu)*	2014		
8	Ma'di *(Okollo)*	2014		

Conclusion:
Today, there are over 1.1 million Lugbarati speakers (2014 census report). The Lugbara Bible is among the top 5 best-selling Bibles distributed by the Bible Society of Uganda. Thanks to the Bible Society of Uganda for this great work, the Lugbara Bible is widely used and accepted across the country and beyond. It has never been revised since 1966. Now God dwells among the Lugbara and He speaks Lugbarati.

We give glory to God for his word translated into the heart language of the people in the West Nile region. Now we have four Bibles, two New Testaments and two portions in all the languages spoken in the region. Language is very dynamic; the Lugbara language has over the years evolved and it is certain that the Lugbara Bible needs revision or a new edition to address meaningfully the needs of the Lugbara Church today. It is therefore the responsibility of the Church in West Nile to determine the need for the new Lugbara Bible edition, to pray for the work and to support it.

We give credit to AIM and CMS for championing the vision for Bible Translation in Uganda and particularly in the West Nile region. Through Bible Translation, we have seen the victory of Jesus and the glory of God shining brightly in the region and across the country. Now we have the Jesus film in several local languages in West Nile region, audio scriptures and online Scriptures for use across the world and on smart phone applications.

The hope for the future is a transformed socio-economic and religious community life in the West Nile region, and Uganda at large, by and through the powerful word of God.

To God Be the Glory

Chapter 10
The Church and Education in Madi and West Nile Diocese
by Juliet Zilly Paratra

The Church in Madi and West Nile Diocese was founded way back in 1918. The missionaries who established churches also started village schools to teach people to read and write, so that the people could read the Scriptures. The education institutions have since grown to many primary, secondary, tertiary institutions and universities. The church-founded education institutions have produced many important men and women who serve this country in various offices both within and abroad. This chapter does not cover every education institution and its products, but what is here is representative enough, as more may come in other editions.

The first schools in Mvara Mission were Arua Boys' Primary School and Mvara Girls' Primary School. Later on, Arua Primary School gave way to Arua Junior Secondary in 1950. Due to lack of space, the Church authorities decided that Arua Boys' Primary School should be moved to Jiako, about 6 kilometers North West of Mvara in 1953. The Girls' School moved off completely in 1954, when it gave way to the Girls' Domestic Science School, *(popularly known as Dom Girls' School)* and no school was left as a demonstration school. In 1952, the Church Authorities started another co-education school, as the Demonstration School for Arua Teacher Training College.

In this same year, a new school, known as Red Land Primary School came into being. It first grew from P6 to P8. Brigadier Barnabas Kili (RIP), the former Minister of Education in Idi Amin Dada's regime, was one of the learners in Red Land Primary School. The school occupied two sites, the old Mvara Girls' Primary school for classes 4, 5 and 6, which became known as Upper Demonstration Primary, and the Red Land Primary School, or Lower Demonstration School for classes 1, 2, 3, and 7.

Many prominent people in Madi and West Nile Diocese and in the nation, passed through these schools. Some of the notable are: Hon. Dr. Eric Adriko, Prof. Stephen Togboa Tikodri, Olara Otunnu, Lt. Col. John Onaah, Canon Gloria Royce Androa and Lulua Odu.

Background of Arua TTC.
In 1931 the AIM missionary Archdeacon Rev. Albert Vollor started Arua Teacher Training College (TTC) and his wife Mrs. Florence Vollor became the first white principal. Arua TTC evolved through these five major phases: Elementary/Normals school in the year 1923-1945, Vernacular Teacher Training College (VTTC) 1946-1951, Grade II TTC between 1953-1982, Grade III from 1983 to date, and in 1998 it achieved Core Primary Teachers' College status.

Vernacular Teacher Training College (VTTC) 1946-1952
The college changed into VTTC as a result of the Protectorate Government policy of improving the standard of education and training of vernacular teachers. They also aimed at opening more TTCs nearer to communities. One way of doing this was to raise the standard of teacher training colleges. By this time, there was only one VTTC for Protestants at Boroboro, which started after the upgrading of elementary school to P.5, because some teachers had already trained in Makerere to grade A and B standard. Qualification for recruitment was from P.6 to teach in village church schools. The grades were V in 1947 which later changed to Grade 1 in 1953.

Arua TTC grade II Training College:
In 1953, Arua TTC was upgraded to grade II status to train students for 4 years, leading to the award of grade II teachers' certificate. This programme went on until 1982 when grade II course was phased out in the country. Arua TTC produced very important people, who have been known nationally and internationally. Some of these people include: Bishop Henry Luke Orombi, Rev. Can. Dr. John Milton Anguyo, Canon John Y Ondoma, Canon Isaac Jaffer Anguyo.

Arua PTC grade III training college: The government White Paper on education 1992 confirmed the upgrading of PTCs. From 1983 to 1985, the grade II teachers' certificate course was phased out completely, and grade III teachers' course was introduced. Entry to the grade 111 teachers' course required an O level certificate with 6 passes, English and Mathematics being compulsory. Another qualification was evidence of teaching for three years as a grade II certified and registered teacher. On the other hand, to qualify for the admission to the in-service course, one must have either passed a minimum of four ordinary level subjects including Mathematics and English, and he/she must have been teaching as a licensed teacher in primary school for at least 3 years.

Church of Uganda Primary Schools: The Primary Schools which are Church of Uganda founded have continued to produce people who served and are serving the church and the nation in big positions. I wish to mention a few of such schools:

Etori Primary School in Arua Archdeaconry was started in 1946, as a village school, and the following prominent persons went through it: Dr. Asea Godfrey and Mrs. Angucia Josephine.

Ombokoro Primary School in Arua Archdeaconry was started in the year 1952. Many people attained primary education in Ombokoro and most of them became successful, including Andama George and Bishop Charles Collins Andaku.

Alua Primary School, which started in 1952, produced Dr. Wilson Enzama, Canon Obeti Bob, Venerable Canon Captain Fanuel Onzima.

Jiako Primary School, which started in 1953, produced the following people: Rt. Hon. Dr. Eric Tiyo Adriko, Engineer Olivu, Nahori Oyaa.

Endru Primary School which started as a village school in 1935 produced: Hon. Engineer Andruale Awuzu, Anguandia Dickens, Samson Ayub Geria.

Anyavu Primary School started in 1936, and gave birth to Anyavu SS. It was started as a village school by a church teacher who didn't know how to read and write. This school produced Jason Avutia, Dribia Gard and Bishop Ephraim Adrale.

Chapter 11
The History of Health Services in West Nile
by Heather Sharland

For over two millennia, Christians, inspired by the example and teaching of Jesus, have been at the forefront of efforts to alleviate human suffering, cure disease, and advance knowledge and understanding of health. Jesus of Nazareth taught: 'Whatever you did for one of the least of these brothers of mine, you did for me.' (Matthew 25:40)

From the very beginning, the Church believed that health care was an important way of bringing practical care to people, and a means of showing God's love. It is not surprising, as we read the history of health care in West Nile, to find that, due to their commitment to love and serve those weaker than themselves as Christ did, people of faith were at the forefront of advancing standards of clinical medicine and patient care.

Kuluva Hospital
The story of how the first medical missionaries to West Nile, Dr Ted and Muriel Williams, came to West Nile, and established the hospital at Kuluva, has been told in an earlier chapter of this book. Soon after the hospital opened in 1951, the leprosy centre was full, as they only had capacity for 100 clients. Small leprosy villages were established in the community, and treatment was given at the hospital on a daily basis.

In 1958 the West Nile District Council introduced bylaws to control leprosy. Basically these were very simple, consisting of rules to compel people thought to be suffering from leprosy to attend for examination and diagnosis, and to make it compulsory for persons diagnosed as having leprosy to attend for treatment. There was a punishment inserted into the bylaws, namely a fine of ten shillings only. This fine has been applied on relatively few occasions. This really helped to control leprosy, and at one stage there were over 4250 patients registered with leprosy. Treatment proved to be very effective, and many were discharged back to their home villages.

In 1990 Dr Richard Ayres started community-based treatment with funds from German Leprosy Relief Association (GLRA). All the patients were integrated back into their home communities. Today there is a small number of People Affected by Leprosy (PALS) with complications under care at the hospital. In 2017, two new patients were enrolled on treatment, and in 2018 one case has been enrolled from Kiryandongo district.

To help with the rehabilitation of the leprosy patients, a workshop was started to make shoes to support their feet and prevent injury. Over 1000 patients have received supportive footwear. This later developed into a workshop to make artificial limbs for amputees, and callipers for people with polio. In 2007 this further developed into an orthopaedic workshop, with support from the Rotary Club. They installed equipment, trained orthopaedic staff in the Jaipur technology, and supplied sufficient materials for an initial 300 limbs.

In the early days of medical care, diseases of the eye were not very high on the priority list, and received very little attention. Dr Peter Williams, when he started working, noticed many patients with eyes problems. Much of the eye work he was involved with was preventing blindness, particularly in those suffering from trachoma and onchocerciasis (river blindness), and giving sight back to the older patients with cataracts.

A young doctor, Dr Keith Waddell, came to Kuluva with these words very much on his mind, *'And God is able to bless you abundantly, so that in all things at all times, having all that you need, you will abound in every good work.'*
(2 Corinthians 9:8)

These were the words prayed over Keith Waddell in his commissioning service in 1964, as he prepared to go out to the mission field. In the early years, under Idi

Amin, Keith was 'the' Doctor, doing 'anything and everything' as he sought to serve Ugandans in the best ways possible. Through his work, like Dr Peter Williams, he saw the need for a specialist eye surgeon in Uganda. He observed that many of the eye problems and blindness he encountered were treatable or preventable. Keith came back to the UK, re-trained in eye work and then headed back to Uganda. Although he was not based at Kuluva, he has been coming annually to the hospital for the last 45 years to treat eye problems.

In the early 1990s, CBM (Christoffell Blinden Mission) assisted Kuluva in the mass treatment of onchocerciasis (River Blindness). This has led to the eradication of river blindness in the area. To achieve VISION 2020, Initiative Medoptics came in 2014, renovated and equipped a room to have a static eye clinic, and to develop comprehensive clinical outreach. Today the eye clinic is offering quality eye services, and refractions are done to identify and support those who need spectacles for reading.

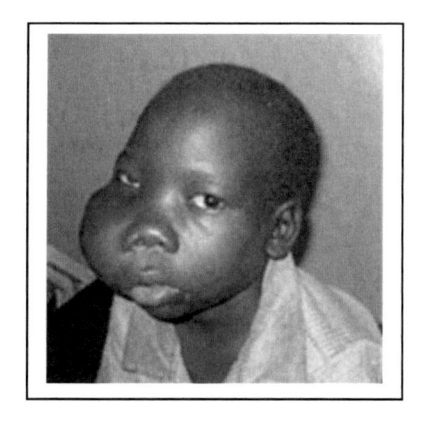

In the 1960s and 70s, Dr Williams, and his friend Dr Burkitt, played a key role in a large field study examining the link between Epstein–Barr virus and the development of Burkitt's Lymphoma, a very disfiguring cancer of the face. Kuluva was chosen as a study centre as West Nile had the highest incidence of Burkitt's Lymphoma in Uganda. The hospital became a centre for visiting researchers from around the world, all intent on studying Burkitt's Lymphoma.

These studies led to the discovery of the association of childhood Epstein Barr Virus infection with the risk of developing Burkitt's Lymphoma and, most importantly, the curative treatment of Burkitt's Lymphoma was discovered. Up until 2017, research was still being carried out at Kuluva, this time by the Emblem project (the Epidemiology of Burkitt's Lymphoma in East African

Children and Minors). Forty years later, Kuluva still treats children with Burkitt's Lymphoma, though their team's capacity has been eroded, mostly due to lack of funds.

In the late 1980s and 1990s, when HIV and AIDS were rampant, Kuluva started receiving and managing HIV positive clients. A psycho-social programme, headed by Joel Arumadri, was started to support the families and clients. In June 2005, Kuluva Hospital was accredited as an ART treatment centre by the Ministry of Health. Over the years several partners helped to develop the HIV/AIDS programme, firstly the Inter Religious Council of Uganda, followed by Cardno. Now the Infectious Disease Institute (IDI) of Makerere University is helping to run and implement the programme activities.

Another area of Medicine Kuluva pioneered was the use of natural medicine alongside pharmaceutical medicine. When Dr Ted Williams came to Kuluva, he often used natural medicines alongside the pharmaceutical. Then in the 1990s this work was revitalised with the help of Anamed. They conducted training for nurses, pharmacy assistants and doctors. A special garden was established to grow some of the useful plants. A small production unit was started. Unfortunately, due to lack of funds and supervision the work did not continue.

Over the years Kuluva has been a leading light in many areas of medical care, and has diversified in response to community need. A Community-Based Health Care programme, supported by Tearfund, was established to address some of the preventable health problems in the community. Community health workers were trained on disease prevention awareness, nutrition education to reduce malnutrition, and encouraging participation in immunisation programmes.

Maternal health and newborn care has always been at the forefront at Kuluva Hospital. Even though the maternity unit helped deliver triplets and Siamese twins, many babies were small and premature, and often these babies would die.

The only way to keep them warm was a hot water bottle. In response to this, in 2007 a special care unit for newborn babies was established. The unit was equipped with 10 incubators; this was the first special care facility in the West Nile Region. Today we are still using the same incubators to care for the new born babies!

List of Medical Superintendents

1. Dr Ted Williams, 2. Dr Lulia Johnston, 3. Dr David Morton,
2. Dr Oryama Jakor, 5. Dr Karlfried Neudec, 6. Dr Elgon Obetia,
7. Dr Patrick Kerchan, 8. Dr Ronald Wadria, 9. Dr Hilary Pariyo
10. Dr Alex Atiku

School of Nursing and Midwifery

When Dr Williams started work at Kuluva, he trained local people as dressers to help with treating patients on the wards, care for the leprosy patients and help in outpatients. The Government forbade the giving of certificates

In 1985 when Sister Kim Chung Youn came to Kuluva, she started training nursing assistants. Then in 1988, the training of Midwifery assistants and Community Health assistants commenced. This was to alleviate the chronic shortage of staff in the hospital.

When Sr. Kim arrived she said, "To be honest, I did feel fear, but the very moment I descended from the plane's staircase and stepped onto the red soil, I was overcome with a sense of peace – and this peace hasn't left me since." Sister Kim attributes this peace entirely to God. It is a peace that has kept her through the years of war, and enabled Kim to live and work in a culture that's not her own, learning to speak an entirely new language, all the while living alone –

without any immediate family or a husband. "I never feel fear," she pragmatically said. "Why would I feel fear, when I know why I'm here?!"

In October 1992 the new School of Nursing structure was in place, and was inspected and accredited by the Uganda Nurses and Midwives Council for the training of Certificate in Nursing. The first class commenced in May 1993. Driciru Monica Efia was among the students in the first set trained; now she is principal of the nursing school.

Sr Kim Chung Youn was the first Principal. Anne Apio Avinyia succeeded her and retired in 2017. Sr. Driciru Monica is now the present Principal.

Course	*Starting date*	*Students completed training*
Certificate in Nursing	*May 1993*	*389*
Enrolled Comprehensive Nursing	*November 2004*	*334*
Certificate in Midwifery	*May 2012*	*134*
Diploma in Nursing	*November 2011*	*74*

The hospital faces a struggle every day to serve the community. Dilapidated buildings, inadequate equipment and lack of funding for staff and drugs, all make the achievements of the hospital in providing the care it does nothing short of miraculous. We praise God the hospital has grown over these past 70 years into a complex hospital, offering many services to the community, with an accompanying Primary School, a School of Nursing and Midwifery and hydro-dam.

At present the Diocese of Madi and West Nile is overseeing 6 rural health centres each with their own story of how they started and developed. Kuluva Hospital, and all the health centres, are non-profit making health facilities that provide health care services to all people in the community. All services at the hospital and at the health centres are delivered in a manner that complies with the requirements of the Uganda Protestant Medical Bureau (UPMB) and the Ministry of Health of Uganda.

St. Luke's Katiyi Health Centre III

St Luke's Katiyi H/C III, previously called St Luke's Dispensary Katiyi, was established in 1982, by the Anglican Church Community of Madi Oyibu Archdeaconry in a grass-thatched house. The motivation behind starting the Dispensary was that people did not have any access to health services in the Madi region, as the existing Government health units collapsed during the continued civil wars in 1970's and early 1980's.

It was also a means of uniting the people of Madi Oyibu Archdeaconry. The health unit picked up very well, with full participation from the community. It was a centre for training Community Health Workers and Traditional Birth Attendants. The trained volunteers ran the dispensary, and managed outpatients and maternity units. Once a month, a Doctor's clinic would take place, when the doctor from Kuluva Hospital would come to examine and treat the difficult cases. Due to the strategic position of the Health Facility, it became a centre for the management of Cholera during the outbreak in 1998.

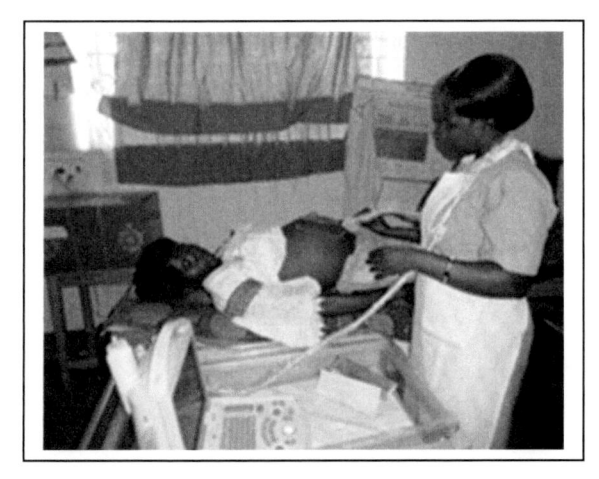

In 2000, Save the Children UK helped with major rehabilitation, improving the outpatient building, then, in 2007, Celia Donald from World Vision UK laid the foundation stone for the children's ward (currently being used as the MCH Block and Maternity). This was the year it was upgraded to a Health Centre III. Over the years, friends, Ministry of Health and UPMB have donated equipment to improve service delivery. In 2016, St. Luke's was given a solar ultrasound, the only health centre in the district to offer ultrasound services for pregnant mothers. In 2016, the health centre was fully accredited by Enabel (BTC) to implement a results based financing project.

Today it is one of the busiest clinics in the Diocese; they see 4587 outpatients per year and deliver 373 babies. In 2017 they were recognised as one of the best-performing Health Centre in Arua District.

Anyiribu Health Centre III

The clinic was established as a rural health post after the liberation war in 1979, supported by the Anglican Church in Peera. In 1980, Akende G Pious started moving from house to house with drugs. In 1981, the Rev Zibidayo Nguma offered his house as a community care point. A small building was erected to be a service centre for treatment and a store for drugs. Three nurse aides were trained to help with service delivery.

In 1986, World Vision built two permanent structures to be used as MCH and outpatients, laboratory and store for drugs. Three grassed-thatched houses were built to be used as inpatient wards. It became a centre for training Community Health Workers and Traditional Birth Attendants, who helped with the delivery of babies. World Vision had a major emphasis on children, and facilitated a child programme at the health centre.

The facility still remains the only health centre in the sub county. In 2016, the facility was partially accredited by Enabel (BTC). This was a learning experience as they pointed out some important gaps in the service delivery at the facility. The in-charge said, "The gaps were things we were already taught in school but hadn't really been implemented yet in our health facility. For example: space between the beds, curtains on the windows and screens between beds for the privacy of patients, hand washing, following all the steps in treatment protocol (take temperature, take blood pressure, take weight,…) They also encouraged us to set flat fee rates, this really helps the clients to know the amount of money to bring to the clinic for treatment."

Then in 2017 the health facility was fully accredited by Enabel (BTC) to implement the results based financing project. RBF specifically focuses on quality improvement at the facility.

Anyavu Health Centre II

Anyavu was the dream of Bishop Ephraim Adale; he wanted to bring health services closer to his people. The clinic started on church land, but it was soon realized that a bigger area of land was needed. The clinic moved to the present site in 2004. Albert Feisel, the engineer from Kuluva, oversaw the design and building of the clinic, and the community raised the funds for the work.

Over the years it has struggled, due to weak leadership, but we believe it can move forward and get its Grade III status soon.

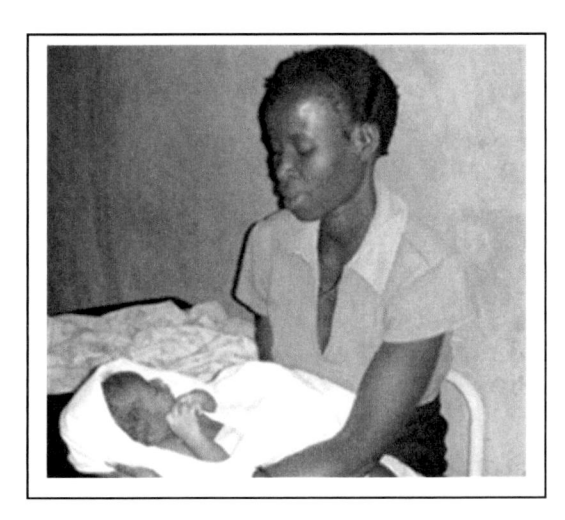

A young nurse, who recently qualified as an Enrolled comprehensive nurse at the Health Centre, said "The beautiful thing about my job is helping a woman becoming a mother, from the first time the mother visits the health facility until she gives birth, I love helping her. It is also a very joyful moment when you see a very sick patient pull through. When you help them to recover and they can go home, taking up their everyday activities. This to me is the most rewarding aspect of my job."

Erepi Health Centre II

The health centre started in 1990 as a dream of the Archdeacon, in the old CMS house. Mr Dramgbu Emin was sent to nursing school, and returned in 1995 with some drugs. He started a drug store and nursing home to serve the community. Due to lack of supervision and management the clinic collapsed.

In 1997 the clinic was revived, with help from Kuluva Hospital when a new Archdeacon came into position. It was registered with the Ministry of Health in 1998. The OPD block was built on the new site, with a loan from Moyo SACCO. The Health Centre was run by nursing aides, and in 1999 one of the nursing aides, Mary Ayise, was sent to Kuluva for nurse training. She came back and was the in-charge of the facility from 2010.

Mr Rokani Charles came as the in-charge in 2011; he had a special interest in MCH (Maternal and Child Health) with a focus on family planning. For several years, Erepi was the best performing health centre in the district on family planning. Staff were trained by Blue Star Marie Stopes as Community Based Distributors, and Erepi was the first clinic in the district to offer Cervical Cancer Screening Services. Today the Health Centre struggles to maintain good clinical services due to the lack of funds.

Yivu Abea Health Centre II

This is the youngest Health Centre in Madi and West Nile Diocese. It all started with a few people in the community having a desire to bring health services closer to the people. Community members would walk 8-12km searching for health care. They dreamt and prayed for many years that a health centre would be built on the church land. God answered their prayers in 2002, under the Community HIV/AIDS Initiative (CHAI).

The community contributed bricks, poles and labour to help build the day care centre. When CHAI was phased out, they left the church with an unfinished 3-roomed building previously constructed as a day care centre. They took the initiative, amidst economic challenges, to finish the building to use as their dream health centre. With technical advice from Dr. Patrick Kerichan, the dream of having a health centre was fully realized in January 2009.

Since then many developments have taken place, a new Maternity and Neonatal ward was built in 2013. There are extensions to the inpatient ward and store room. Ground has been broken for the building of another inpatient ward. The facility was accredited as a grade III Health Centre in 2016. They were accredited by BTC (ENABEL) in 2016 to start results based financing. Their aim is to become a Grade IV within the first decade of the 2nd century of Christianity in West Nile.

The Christian ethos is very much at the centre of all their developments. They really appreciated Global Link Africa, for supporting the Health Centre with young professional Christian missionaries. Komakech Simon was one of the first group of young missionaries, a clinical officer whom God really called to serve; he remained and became the in-charge of the health centre. His Christian witness has been amazing to other staff and community around.

Kei Health Centre III

Kei Health Centre III started as a dispensary in 1994 in a grass-thatched house after the Diocesan Council declared that projects needed to be established in parishes.

Shortly afterwards a team from Kuluva Hospital and Here is Life went to Kei Parish, and they were shown a vast bush area that was so fertile. Canon Baba Nikula and the team had dreamt of what could become of this area. Under the chairmanship of Ondoga Fenasi, the construction started with support from Here is Life.

In 2000 the construction was completed and the Health Centre officially opened in February 2001. Birgit Klump of CFI came to live at Kei and start the clinical work at Kei. She had a passion for Community Health Evangelism (CHE) and a very strong community health education programme was established, with volunteers walking from home to home with vigour. Due to insecurity in the area and other missionaries being killed, Birgit's time in Kei was shortened, and she left in 2004. The Health centre continued to function under leadership of Ugandan Clinical officers and nurses.

In 2008, Here is Life handed the management of the health centre to Madi & West Nile Diocese. There were a few shaky years when the community had a negative attitude towards the health centre and drug supplies were not sufficient. ENABEL (BTC) came timely to support faith-based facilities in the West Nile Region if they reached the required standards for accreditation. We praise God that Kei reached the standards, and in 2017 received medical equipment and a start-up supply of drugs to start on RBF (Result Based Financing). Kei also is a centre for UHMG (Uganda Health and Marketing Group) to trial the voucher system for health care.

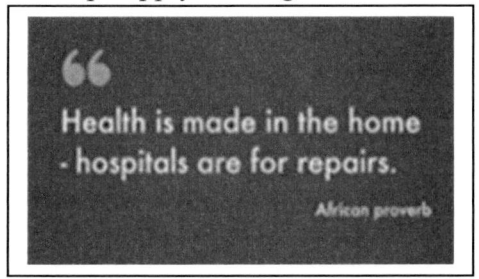

> Health is made in the home - hospitals are for repairs.
> African proverb

We believe that the basis for all health care should be a blend of curative and preventative care, balanced with biblical instruction. Therefore, as a Diocese, we have a Christ-Centred community health education programme that equips the community to identify issues, looks at ways sustainable change can take place and lives are transformed.

One such programme is Wise Choices for Life, which empowers vulnerable men and women in the child-bearing age group with reproductive health knowledge and skills to break the poverty cycle. The lack of information and understanding of reproductive and maternal health in these areas is one of the root causes of poverty.

It's imperative to look after mothers so they can give birth to a healthy child and be fit to care for them. The importance of antenatal care, preparing for birth, and caring for the newborn child are all vital elements of our training. Breast feeding, immunization, and healthy, balanced diets for mother and child as they grow, all contribute to the health of both mother and child. All this comes together in the 1st 1000 days of a child's life.

As we look forward to the next centenary, we pray as a Church we will walk alongside people, demonstrating the love, mercy and compassion our faith demands, transforming the health of children and their families in West Nile. Christians have consistently raised the social status of the weak, sick and handicapped, and sought to love and care for them to the utmost of their abilities. West Nile Christians have been pioneers in research and ethics, in promoting increased standards of care, and in immunology, public health and preventative medicine.

Christianity gives men and women a new perspective and allegiance; their lives are spent in grateful service of the God who has redeemed them and given them new life. In many ways, Christianity and medicine are natural allies; medicine gives men and women unique opportunities to express their faith in daily practical caring for others, embodying the commands of Christ:

"Whatever you did for one of the least of these brothers of mine, you did for me." Matthew 25:40

Chapter 12
The Church and Socio-Economic Development
by Jackson Atria and Christopher Yiki Ondia

1. Introduction
Socio-economic development is the process of social and economic development in a society. It incorporates activities involving both social and economic factors, which result in the growth of the economy and in societal progress, and is measureable in both economic and social terms.

The Church of Uganda has been active in socio-economic Development in the country since the coming of the missionaries in the late 19th century. The focus of the missionaries was health and education, and they introduced these services through institutions that were established in different parts of the country. These were later handed over to the Church of Uganda in the 20th century, when the missionaries left, and they continue to be among the best health and educational facilities in the country up to this day.

In the 1960s and 1970s the church championed socio-economic development through its Christian Rural Service (CRS) programme, and later through the Planning, Development and Rehabilitation (PDR) department. PDR now works through all the Dioceses in the Province of the Church of Uganda to deliver socio-economic programmes to communities at the grassroots level.

2. Church of Uganda and Socio-Economic Development

PDR was established at a time when the country was experiencing political, social and economic turmoil. It was a response in fulfilment of Christ's mission "...I have come that they may have life, and have it to the full." (John 10:10). Since then, PDR's mandate has grown and it has been championing the Church of Uganda's response to the development challenges which are faced by various communities in the Province. The development of its first strategic plan in 2012, further transformed PDR into a facilitator of socio-economic development interventions of the Church, focusing on cross-cutting issues such as gender, HIV/AIDS mainstreaming, malaria prevention and control, disaster risk reduction and emergency response, population growth and control, promoting peace and social justice. PDR also set out to strengthen household capacities in water, food and income security across communities, as well as augmenting the capacity of church insititutions and structures, from the grass roots to national levels.

In 2017, following the approval of the first ever Church of Uganda Provincial strategic plan, PDR was rebranded, and is now known as the Directorate of Household and Community Transformation. This has become the social services arm of the Church of Uganda. Since its formation, the Directorate has focused its work on the fight against poverty, disease, illiteracy, injustice, and the marginalization of the poor in society. The Directorate implements a "bottom-up" community development strategy. Families are to be empowered at household level, through their community organizations, so that they take charge of their own development agenda. This was to improve their quality of life irrespective of their faith, sex, tribe, or ethnicity. The aim of the programme is to make local communities and Church of Uganda institutions self-reliant in their day to day requirements. Its emphasis is on building their capacity to enable them to identify and prioritise their challenges/needs, act to reduce poverty and hunger, and promote good health among the people of God.

3. Madi and West Nile Diocese and Socio-Economic Development
The socio-economic development history of the West Nile region is unique, as it was originally part of the Belgian Congo, and only became part of the British Protectorate during the re-demarcation of Africa in 1914. The British did not have a high regard for West Nile people; they imagined that unlike the organized Bantu, the inhabitants of the West Nile region were only good at providing unskilled labour. There were no serious government socio-economic development programmes. West Nile became a labour reserve to supply unskilled labour to the sugar plantations in Buganda and Bunyoro regions. Because of their physique, the West Nile people also became valuable as recruits for the King's African Rifles.

As a result of its addition to colonial Uganda, West Nile was one of only three areas of Uganda that had not been touched by missionary work. The Church Missionary Society (CMS) had already over-extended itself in the evangelistic thrust of the previous twenty years. Protestant Christianity was therefore introduced to West Nile by the Africa Inland Mission (AIM) in 1918, as has been described in earlier Chapters of this book. The work of the AIM missionaries concentrated on spreading the gospel and winning souls for Christ, and did little to uplift the socio-economic status of the natives. It was only in 1923, with the arrival of Albert and Florence Vollor, that the ministry of the missionaries was boosted and uplifted through education.

This changed the fortunes of the people in West Nile. In addition to opening worship centers, the missionaries began to introduce education and modern health care services within the West Nile region, to help improve the socio-economic status of the region. The missionaries founded schools, which included Mvara Junior School, which became Mvara Senior Secondary, and Goli Junior Secondary, and many other primary or junior secondary schools. These became some of the best schools in the region. Besides the educational facilities, the missionaries also established health institutions, the biggest in West Nile being Kuluva Hospital, which has to this day maintained its missional and holistic approach in providing both spiritual and physical healing.

In the late 1960s and early 1970s, with the creation of Madi and West Nile Diocese out of the Diocese of Northern Uganda in 1969, the church started championing socio-economic development, through the Christian Rural Service (CRS) programme. Christian Rural Service workers were recruited, trained and deployed in all parishes, to support rural farmers to improve agricultural productivity for enhanced food and income security, and supported programmes to improve community hygiene and adult literacy. The programme also gave hope to the marginalised and uprooted persons within the region, such as refugees from Rwanda, Congo, South Sudan, and Kenya.

But this programme would only be short-lived and collapsed as a result of the socio-economic instability experienced in the country during the Idi Amin era. The process of removing Idi Amin Dada, and the social and political instability that followed his removal, meant that the Church of Uganda, especially in the West Nile region, could not continue to carry out any development work. West Nile was the region Amin came from, and the region where the war to end his regime was most brutal. Most people had to flee into exile in DRC and South Sudan.

Even as people slowly began to come back from exile, the sporadic rebel activities of the UNRF and West Nile Bank Front caused half of the population in the region to move from their homes, and return to exile or in Internally Displaced Camps, from the early 1990s until as late as 2001. As the people were starting to recover from exile, the rebel activities of the Lord's Resistance Army in the Acholi region (1986-2005), led to the loss of lives and property of many people of the Diocese during their travel to and from Kampala.

During this whole period, the focus of the Church's work in the region shifted from development to rehabilitation. As many people returned from exile or Internally Displaced Camps, they came back to a life of total deprivation as all economic resources, social ties and safety nets had been destroyed. The people's ability to do things for themselves was severely eroded.

This period (1980s and 90s) was when the Department of Planning, Development and Rehabilitation at the Provincial level worked actively and closely with the Madi and West Nile Diocese. Initially, this was to support the rehabilitation and resettlement effort, to enable the process of people rebuilding their lives to take place. But the focus later turned to socio-economic development, as people took control of their lives, especially from the late 1990s.

Indeed, from that time, many projects were funded by various development partners and donors, through the Planning, Development and Rehabilitation unit of Church of Uganda, and implemented in Madi West Nile Diocese. These were aimed at addressing the socio-economic needs of the people. Various churches, parishes and individuals have benefited from projects in the areas of peace and reconciliation, agriculture, nutrition and food security, livelihood, environmental protection, including tree planting, water and sanitation, education, and gender based violence, all implemented by the Health, Education and Planning and Development Departments of the Diocese.

In line with changes at the provincial level, with effect from this year 2018, the Diocese has introduced a new Department of Household and Community Transformation which will take full responsibility for socio-economic transformation of households and communities through a process approach. The main thrust of the work will be to effect mind change and empower people, through the various structures of the church, to take control of their socio-economic needs across the whole diocese.

4. Key development challenges: By and large however, the impact of the various development interventions on the people has been limited. Socio-economic challenges, including poverty, have not only remained a reality in the lives of many West Nilers, but poverty continues to deepen. We believe there are a number of reasons for this.

For many years the region repeatedly experienced one cycle of political and social instability after another, leading to insecurity. This affected people's ability to engage effectively in socio-economic activities. This also meant that the Church could not sustainably improve the socio-economic status of the people, through community empowerment programmes. The focus of the socio-economic development interventions have not been on empowering people to do things for themselves, but on providing for them through various projects. These projects have not only fragmented development efforts, but have actually helped to disempower people, and make them dependent on external help.

Moreover, the colonial policy of making West Nile a labour reservoir for recruiting labourers for estates, plantations and farms in the south, has had a lasting impact on the people. Even today, people still continue to flock to these farms and plantation for employment. Most security guards in Kampala, and the other large urban centres, still come from this region. Added to this, the Africa Inland Mission missionaries were focused on evangelism and not so much on economic development. Indeed revival took over riches, good dressing, jewellery, education, etc as these were considered signs of not being saved, in some fellowship groups of the revivals. Names like "Ayikobua" meaning 'happiness is in heaven', are common among saved Christians from this region, because they believed that Christianity was supposed to be preparing people for heaven only.

The biggest problem, however, seems to be the mindset and attitude of the people. Before our people were forced to go into exile, West Nilers were very hard-working, and believed in earning whatever they needed for their livelihood.

They were very proud people, who would never take what did not belong to them. Indeed West Nilers had many other gifts and great attributes such as resilience, which is strength in weakness, hard-working, being diligent and determined and pressing on, despite all odds, trust worthiness and honesty. But a lot of these attributes were lost when they were forced into a life of dependency in refugee camps. We have failed to recover from this tragedy, and have not made use of and maximized the positive attributes of the people. Instead of being proud, many of our people are ashamed, and now walk with their heads down. Dependency syndrome is very common, and we believe we are poor and incapable, and therefore cannot do without external help in the form of 'projects'.

Some traditional and cultural beliefs have not helped our cause either. Many people from West Nile believe that what they own is for all in the clan or community. It should be shared, so that no one is left to suffer, even when they have made no effort to do anything for themselves. Many blame others for their misfortune, as they believe that when they fail to make it in life, it is because those who are rich have taken everything from them, or because their families are not supporting them. Indeed, some believe that when they get rich, they will be bewitched, or that they fail in business because they have been cursed. Today, very few Christians are taking advantage of government programmes for economic empowerment. We can count the number of Christians in Arua who have progressive businesses. They are few, and this historical background has remained with the Christians in Madi and West Nile Diocese until now.

5. The Way Forward
We believe that the solution is in changing mind sets, empowering people and helping them to regain hope, belief and courage to do things for themselves. Our people should be helped to rediscover their lost attributes. The Church can play a huge role here, not through one-off projects, but through a persistent long-term action-learning process. This involves working closely with the people over a long period of time, sharing their challenges and learning together with them from these challenges. Intervention strategies can be agreed and improved on an

ongoing basis, taking into consideration the lessons learnt, and changes within the wider environment. The Household and Community Transformation unit will be a good vehicle for this, but the Church will also need to be strategic in mobilising local resources. We need to put into effect rigorous planning, and to strengthen our structures to establish strategic partnerships for long term change.

Chapter 13
The Church and Politics by Harold E. Acemah

The Church and politics have had an uneasy relationship for many years; they have, at best, enjoyed peaceful co-existence in Uganda since the 1950s. I remember when I was a student at Ombatini Junior Secondary (1959-1960), our teachers regularly warned us sternly keep clear of politics, because politics, according to them, was a dirty and dangerous game. At thirteen years old, I did not even know what 'politics' was, except for rumours we heard about two organizations called Congress and DP (Democratic Party). During the 1950s and 1960s, politics was "banned" in schools, whatever that means.

After Independence, talk about politics being a dirty game sort of died down. Schools became fertile recruitment grounds for politicians, who turned their attention to the churches, which were and still are the most influential and credible organized institutions in Uganda. Aware of the fact that a word or two from church leaders about a political issue can have positive or negative consequences, politicians started to make a noise and argue loudly that organized church should keep out of politics, which is impossible, undesirable and unnecessary.

What our political leaders mean is that the Church as an institution should keep out of partisan politics. In the case of the Church of Uganda (CoU), which has historically been associated with the Uganda Peoples Congress (UPC), some Ugandan politicians have demanded the CoU should not directly or indirectly support UPC. This unfair and unreasonable demand would, needless to mention, deny Church leaders their human and constitutional right to participate as individuals in the affairs of a country of which they are bona fide or legitimate citizens.

What is Church?
The word church is first used in Matthew 16 verse 18 where Jesus told his disciples: "And I tell you that you are Peter and on this rock I will build my church and the gates of Hades (hell) will not overcome it."

The church is not a building. Christians *are* the church. Church is the believers in Christ or the body of Christ (Colossians 1:24) and without Christians there is no church. Jesus Christ is the head of the church (Ephesians 5:22) and the church exists wherever there are Christians.

What is Politics?
Politics began its long and checkered history as a term of abuse for activities of those engaged in factions, and gradually became respectable as modern forms of representation evolved. This may explain why politics is often condemned as a dirty game.

Isaac D'Israeli, a British politician, defined politics cynically as "the art of governing mankind through deceiving them." Lord Butler, another British politician, called politics "the art of the possible", a description which is popular with many contemporary politicians. For the ancient Greek philosopher Aristotle, politics is the "master science", in the sense that it gives all other sciences some priority and order in their rival claims to the scarce resources of any given community or society. He argued that politics is only one possible solution to the challenge and problem of order. It is by no means the most common, but on balance, it is much better than tyranny and oligarchy.

The concept of power is central in virtually all definitions of politics. Max Weber's definition, which is often cited by political scientists, brings this out clearly. According to Weber, "Politics for us means striving to share power or striving to influence the distribution of power, either among states or among groups within a state." In other words, power is the capacity to allocate resources; no wonder the struggle for power in Uganda, Kenya, Rwanda, Burundi, DR Congo and South Sudan, since the advent of independence, has been so bloody and so costly in material terms, but especially in terms of human suffering and lives lost.

Since most politicians are driven by their desire or lust for power, they have turned the political arena into a battle ground, where the winner takes all, and the loser must hide, run for safety or bite the dust. Politics in Africa, including Uganda, has sadly become a 'do or die' activity, which has led *wananchi* to conclude that politics is a dirty game, which a decent, respectable and value-driven organization like the Church should keep out of.

There are two competing schools of thought about the role of the Church in politics, and both claim to derive their authority and legitimacy from Scripture. One school of thought believes that the Church should not play any role in politics, while the other, to which I belong, believes that the Church and Church leaders, in their personal capacity as citizens, have a legitimate and important role to play in politics. The second school includes those who preach "Liberation Theology."

Can the Church afford to be silent?
Against the background of several burning social, economic and political questions facing Uganda and Africa today, can the Church afford to be silent? Can the Church afford to keep quiet, fold its hands and do nothing? I believe it is critical for the Church, as well as Christians in their individual capacities, to stand up and speak clearly, and let their voices be heard.

As people of faith prepare positions on political issues, or as they prepare to cast their votes at national or local elections, it is necessary for the Church to take a stand within the laws of the country, and educate the believers in accordance with our Christian principles and teachings.

The Church can educate and guide members of congregation on particular pieces of legislation or topical issues. The Church can do the following: the Church can receive and distribute non-partisan voter education materials; the Church can allow candidates for elections, and duly elected officials, to speak on relevant issues during Church services; Churches can educate members of their congregation on pending Bills before Parliament, or draft pieces of legislation before Local Councils. The Clergy can privately support and vote for particular candidates during elections. Churches should **not** make donations to political parties or candidates for political campaigns.

Chapter 14
The Most Difficult Times the Diocese Has Gone Through by Canon Isaac Jaffer Anguyo

The years from 1979 to 2007 are best termed the most difficult and dark times for the Madi and West Nile Diocese, due to both outside challenges and internal conflicts. Firstly, the overthrow of Idi Amin's government and the reprisal killings which followed, forced many to hide in remote areas and many more went into exile in DR Congo and Sudan. These are also known as the 'lost years', especially for school age children. Many had a hard 'camp experience', away from their homes, receiving free food and being looked after by the UN. Even following the resettlement and rehabilitation programmes, the provision of 'Relief Aid' has continued to impact the lives of the people in places where few have work and many still expect free things.

The Church of Uganda Christians still mourn those killed in the massacres in Muni and Ringili, and Catholic Christians still remember the Ombaci massacre.

The people thought they would find safety and security in their Christian institutions, but death followed them to the altars. Many were left with unanswered questions, "Where is God? Why is there all this suffering?"

These could be called outside challenges. Some saw them as the work of the enemy of the Church. But the internal conflicts in the Madi and West Nile Diocese almost tore the church into pieces. Thank God that the 2001 events, which are summarized below, largely ended in the Church coming together in a reconciliatory spirit, although the effects are still felt in some parts of Arua Archdeaconry.

In 2001, a crisis took place in which the Church was divided into two parts in conflict; the Madi and West Nile Diocese headed by Bishop Enock Lee Drati, and the Arua Archdeaconry headed by Venerable Gresham Draku. Arua Archdeaconry actually tried to leave the Madi and West Nile Diocese and to create their own diocese.

This was expressed in a letter to the Archbishop of the Church of Uganda, signed by the Head of the Laity of the Arua Archdeaconry. Part of the letter reads:
> '... the only solution, which is now the "felt need" of all the Christians, is that God is bringing all these upon people who have supported the Diocese with their soul, mind and strength, and yet time has come for not appreciating them, is that Arua Archdeaconry be granted a Diocese in the future.'

The members of Arua Archdeaconry set out their grievances. They had given their property for the establishment of Madi and West Nile Diocese, but the Archdeaconry had been relegated to the smallest part of the office block. The Archdeaconry had worked harmoniously with all the previous bishops, Bishop Wani, Bishop Remelia, Bishop Adrale and Bishop Nguma. But when it came to the time of Bishop Drati, they felt that he had overturned all that the previous Bishops had done.

They accused him of transferring their headquarters to Jiako, where there were no facilities, and of saying at St. Paul's Theological College on June 10, 1998 that he would fight the Ayivu spirit of political rivalry to the end. They felt that Bishop Drati was afraid of Venerable Draku, because of the rumours and lies that Draku was responsible for the deaths of the two Bishops. If Draku wanted to become the Bishop of Madi and West Nile Diocese, then Drati did not want to have Draku near him.

The Arua Archdeaconry members also accused Bishop Drati of transferring Ven. Draku from being an Archdeacon to head a parish at Adjumani, a transfer which Draku had refused. The Archdeaconry rejected the leadership of Bishop Drati, and so refused to remit the moneys supposed to go to the diocesan office. They also resolved not to allow Bishop Drati to carry out any confirmations in Arua Archdeaconry. The Arua Archdeaconry claimed they were retaining the church offertories to compensate themselves for the assets which they had left at Mvara, when they were forced to transfer the Archdeaconry offices to Jiako..

In response, the Diocese made counter accusations against the Archdeaconry, and summoned members of Arua Archdeaconry to appear before the Diocesan Tribunal. The Diocese claimed that they were unlawfully performing uncanonical confirmations, thereby usurping the functions of the bishop, that they were causing division among Christians in the Archdeaconry, and even issuing threats to kill church personnel, so that clergy and Christians loyal to the Diocese were under attack. They had authorized their Assets Committee to withhold Arua Archdeaconry contributions to the Diocese, and had attended illegal meetings to prevent the Bishop from exercising his Episcopal powers and duties.

Furthermore, The Diocese claimed that they had obstructed the Bishop, plotted the breakaway of Arua Archdeaconry, refused to attend the Bishop's meetings, instigated violence and disobedience against the Bishop and the Diocesan Secretary. They had told lies against the Bishop, and sent letters claiming to be from others to cause division, hatred, malice and insubordination. They had disrupted church functions, locked churches, and used the local media to obstruct the Bishop's work. They were even accused of becoming polygamous in breach of Canon Law and marriage vows, so bringing the Church into disrepute.

Although it seemed that the whole of the Arua Archdeaconry was involved, in fact, more than ten of their churches had sided with the Diocese. They were threatened, and the Bishop was prevented from confirming their Christians. There was hatred, disunity and lack of Christian love. Even the Revival fellowships were split and organised along Diocesan and Archdeaconry lines. Fighting broke out among the Christians, and others including Catholics and those outside the Church, were drawn into the dispute. Disputes were taken to the Civil Courts, there was no forgiveness and the Bishop even had to have police protection to carry out confirmations in some churches.

The Archbishop sent a delegation to meet the two groups to seek reconciliation, holding meetings of the Clergy on the two sides. These seemed to show that dialogue would bring the needed peace. But the Arua Archdeaconry stood their ground. They would continue to reject Bishop Drati's leadership, unless they were compensated for their assets, the suspension of the clergy and laity was lifted, and the transfers of the 'rebel' clergy revoked.

The Diocese still saw the behaviour of the clergy and some laity as indiscipline, and in breach of Canon Law. The members of Arua Archdeaconry were asked to repent and ask for forgiveness, to accept the leadership of the Bishop and to return the Diocesan money.

With both sides still opposed, the Diocese set up a tribunal to try some clergy and laity who were seen to be disobeying Canon Law, and to be rebels in the Diocese. So the conflict continued. The Arua Archdeaconry was divided into two, with those Christians, Churches and Parishes obedient to the Bishop on one side, and those still opposed to the Bishop and obedient to the Arua Archdeaconry on the other.

But in 2005, Bishop Drati retired, and, to elect the next Bishop, nominations were called from the Archdeaconries. The Arua Archdeaconry had refused to be under Bishop Drati. Should they be allowed to make a nomination? The problem was solved by creating a new Archdeaconry called Adalafu. When the Bishops elected Bishop Obetia to replace Bishop Drati, the Arua Archdeaconry, led by the Ven Draku, came in full force to support the consecration and enthronement. Many from the Arua Archdeaconry saw Bishop Obetia as their bishop.

With Bishop Obetia in office, the Arua Archdeaconry returned to the Diocese without conditions. Ven. Draku was transferred to Vurra, and Ven. Asher Matua was transferred to Arua Archdeaconry. But Bishop Obetia did not recognise the Adalafu Archdeaconry, as the problem was now not between the Diocese and the Arua Archdeaconry, but within the Arua Archdeaconry. Under Bishop Obetia, a section of the Archdeaconry was allowed to create their own Parish, called Ariceni, with three churches and a family church. They preferred to work directly with the Diocese, and not through the leadership of the Arua Archdeaconry.

When Bishop Charles Collins Andaku took office in 2017, he made resolving the old problem his first priority. He visited Ariceni Parish, where the 730 Christians told him that they were still not ready to be under the leadership of the Arua Archdeaconry. After a number of consultations, the Ariceni group were given Parish Status, and made answerable to the Provost of Emanuel Cathedral.

Is this conflict situation unique to the Madi and West Nile diocese? No, many such conflicts have been witnessed throughout the history of the Church. The good thing is that it has now come to a good conclusion. With Ariceni being granted parish status, and being recognized by Bishop Charles Andaku, and Ariceni Parish coming under the supervision of the Cathedral, we are not far from seeing Arua Archdeaconry fully reconciled and able to worship the Lord together in Spirit and in Truth.

Appendix 1: List of Missionaries and Overseas Christians who worked with the Anglican Church in West Nile

(AIM UK: Africa Inland Mission UK; AIM USA: Africa Inland Mission USA; ODA: Overseas Development Agency, UK Govt.; WC: World Concern; LM: Leprosy Mission; CMS UK: Church Mission Society; CMS I: Church Mission Society Ireland; TF: Tear Fund;

Personnel	Dates	Remarks
At Vurra/Ezuku		
Frank and Edith Gardner	1918 - 1919	AIM UK Baptists; See Chapter 3 for full story; with their baby daughter Beryl
Alfred Gardner	1918 - 1919	AIM UK; brother to Frank; came with Frank and Edith
Mr Crowell	1918 - 1919	AIM USA; was with the Gardners and seven other members of the AIM US Group, who moved to wok in Congo
At Mvara		
Mr Mount	1918-1923	Based in Congo but regularly visited Arua
Rev Albert and Florence Vollor	1923-1966	AIM UK; long-serving AIM missionaries in West Nile; See Chapter 4 for full story
Oswald and Grace Stillwell	From 1923	AIM USA
Maurice and Zilla Garner	1934-1938	AIM UK; maternal grandparents of Zilla Whitehouse, now serving at Mbarara
Rev Seton and Peggy (Mary) Maclure	1942-1985	AIM UK; long-serving AIM missionaries in West Nile; see Chapter 4 for full story; worked at Mvara, translation of Lugbara bible with Laura Bell; trained many West Nile clergy
Miss McCard Miss Wightman	1943	AIM UK; both served at Mvara
Miss Barbara Grey	1946	AIM UK; served at Mvara
Douglas and Bettie Thornton	1948-1952	AIM UK; worked at Mvara and at Kuluva as missionary and builder; they had a child who died and was buried in Arua
Rev Donald and Olive Temple	1952-53 1968-72	AIM UK; worked at Mvara with Church; returned to Mvara to work as Chaplain to Bishop Wani; went to Kenya with AIM
Phil Weeks	1960s	AIM UK; served with AIM in Congo, then ran Arua Bookstore
Gordon McCullough	1965	AIM UK; ran Arua Bookstore after Phil Weeks
Nick Gazard	1990s	AIM UK: volunteer on church and school projects for 1 year
Rev Allan & Anne Lacey	2007- 2013	CMS UK; Parish Ministries, Lectionary Link, Reprographics. Health Coordinator.
David and Heather Sharland	2010 -	CMS UK; supporting sustainable agriculture in West Nile, Community Health especislly Girls' Health

Lyn Cooke	2011-2016	AIM UK; Women's Ministry
At Mvara Ecumenical Vocational Training Centre.		
Ernie and Faith Wallace		CMS I; relocated from S. Sudan. Built and established present site
Billy Smyth		CMS I; further developed the Vocational Training.
Aart/Geesje Danbregan		CMS I; from the Netherlands. Strengthened business footing of the centre.
At Arua Teacher Training College		
Stuart and May Cole	1956-1973	AIM UK; son of Stuart Cole Senior who founded Goli. See Chapter 4 for full story
Bertha Vollor	1956-1968	AIM UK; daughter of the Vollors; worked in Arua TTC
Rachel Salmon	1950s-1960s	AIM UK; taught at Arua TTC; married Julian Jackson, served in Kenya
Handel and Joan Bennet	1950-1965	AIM UK; Joan taught at Arua TTC and Handel ran the Arua Bookstore. Also Accountant. From Edgware, London.
Barbara Cottier	1961-1970	AIM UK/ODA; taught at Arua TTC; went to Kenya to train teachers and to be Head of Kitale Primary Boarding School
Barbara Anderson	1966	AIM UK; taught at Arua TTC
Pamela Witts	1960s-1970	AIM UK; taught at Arua TTC
Mvara (with Junior/Senior Secondary Schools		
(Note: all teaching staff switched from AIM to Government contracts after 1962)		
Margaret Lloyd	1946-1979	AIM/ODA; See Chapter 4 for full story; very much involved with the East African Revival and the Balokole movement
Richard (Dick) Gillman	1950 -1953	AIM UK; Head Master, Mvara S.S. Military man, instilled discipline but fair. Insisted on celebrating Remembrance Sunday.
Poppy Agnew	1960s	AIM/ODA; taught Art and Domestic Science at MJSS and MSSS, and Demonstration School
Colin Rockwood	1960s	AIM UK; taught at MSSS as volunteer
Lewis & Angela Stephenson	1960s-1971	AIM/ODA; Headmaster MSSS, taking over from Margaret Lloyd; taught Maths; oversaw massive expansion of school
Christine Walker	1960s-1972	ODA; taught Music and English at MSSS
Stephen Craxton	1960s	AIM UK; volunteer; taught one year at MSSS
Richard Grinstead	1960s	AIM UK; volunteer; taught one year at MSSS
Andrew Dow	1960s	AIM UK; volunteer; taught one year at MSSS; became Rev.
Richard Inwood	1969	AIM UK; volunteer; taught at MSSS; became Bishop
Gordon & Grace McCullough	1968-1970	ODA/AIM; both taught at MSSS, Maths and English

Name	Years	Details
John Martin	1968-1970	ODA; taught English at MSSS
John Haden	1968-1971	ODA/AIM; taught Science at MSSS; supported SU in WN schools
Jenny Peck	1969-1971	ODA/AIM; taught Science at MSSS, now Jenny Haden
Wendy Moore	1971-1973	ODA; taught Maths and Science at MSSS
Christian Rural Services (CRS) at Mvara		
John and Ihla Hooyer	1986-1990	CRWRC. Worked with CRS in Mvara and Farmer Contact groups throughout the Diocese. Died in car accident
Muni Girls School		
Sally Taylor	1984-86	AIM UK; volunteer teacher for two years at Muni
Simon and Clare Martin	1986-1989 1993-2001	AIM UK; taught at Muni Girls' school, then at Mvara /Arua to work with the Church and at Ringili;
Goli and Nebbi		
Harry Hurlburt	1920s	AIM USA; lived near Nebbi in a house in a tree!
Stuart Cole Senior	1929-1938	AIM UK; came from Congo to establish a church centre at Goli
Miss M Moore	Early 1930s	Canadian AIM; taught at Mvara and then moved to Goli
Miss M Quelch	Early 1930s	AIM UK; taught at Goli
Miss Audrey Danby	Early 1930s	AIM UK; taught at Goli
Mr and Mrs John Burse	1938-1946	AIM USA; took over from Coles at Goli, helped to establish dispensary at Goli and then went to Sudan
Miss M Watkins	1930s	AIM UK; Nurse at Goli
Rev Geoffrey Leicester	1948 -1951.	AIM UK. From Bath, England.
Rev and Mrs John Jowett	1958-1962	AIM UK; came as layman then returned as Rev; served at Goli
Rev Bob and Mrs Jean Booth	1960s - 1980s	AIM USA; moved from Sudan to Goli and then move d to Ringili
Sister Kim	From 1986	AIM USA seconded from World Concern; at Kuluva from 1986, moved to Goli;
Sang-Ho and Sue-kueng Paes	1980s	AIM Korea; Scripture Union work in schools;
John and Anne O'Connell	1997-2004	AIM UK; came from Kenya; based at Goli and involved in sustainable agriculture
Nicky Thuambe (née Darby)	1997-2004	Seconded from Crosslinks to AIM; served at Goli and involved in financial administration in Nebbi Diocese
Moyo/Erepi		
Hamilton Wilkes	1936	AIM UK; moved from Karamoja to serve at Moyo/Erepi

Stuart Cole (sen)	1940	AIM UK; moved from Goli to serve in Moyo for one year
Koboko		
Joy Grindey	1962-1996	AIM UK; skilled linguist; based at Mvara then moved to village near Koboko while working on the Kakwa Bible
Ringili near Kuluva		
Rev. Bob and Jean Booth	1980s	AIM USA; moved from Goli to do Boys' Brigade and Church work at Ringili
Laura Belle Barr	1951-1980	AIM USA; see Chapter 4 for full story from 1951; involved in translation of the Lugbara Bible; at Ringili from 1960 onwards
Bill and Myra Hutchinson	1950s-1970s	AIM UK; helped to set up Ringili Vocational School
Paul and Jan Dean	1970s-1980	Worked with Tear Fund based at Ringili
Mark and Dayno Blair	1983-1988	AIM USA; served at Ringili, teaching pastors, then moved to Mukono
Keith & Margaret Rowberry	1985-1987	AIM UK; lived at Mvara; he taught at Ringili
Karan MaWhinney	Early 1980s	AIM UK; from Northern Ireland
Medical Work/Kuluva		
Dr. Ted and Mrs Muriel Williams	1942-1979	AIM UK; came first to Mvara and started a hospital; moved hospital to Kuluva: see Chapter 4 for full story
Miss M Hayward	1945-1950	AIM UK; Nursing at Mvara
Dr Trout	1950s	Doctor at Kuluva
Mr and Mrs J H Williams	1950s - 1965	AIM UK; had been a governent engineer in Kenya; in retirement, came to help build hospital at Kuluva
Margaret Miller	1953-1960s	AIM UK; Nursing at Kuluva
Pat Whisson	1954-1960s	AIM Australia; nursing at Kuluva
Edith Samuels	1954-1960s	AIM Australia; nursing at Kuluva
Miss M Bryant	1954	AIM UK; Nursing at Kuluva
Rev John and Dr Josephine Dobson	1960s	She served with CMS at Kuluva as doctor and he worked with the Church

Dr Keith Waddell	1964 -1965 1982-1987	AIM UK; Served as general doctor at Kuluva 1964-65, see Chapter 5 for full story; then moved to Kagando; returned to Kuluva to serve with Dr Lulua 82-87
Jennifer Burgess	1965-1970	AIM UK; Nursing at Kuluva
Maureen Moore	1966-1986	AIM UK; Nursing at Kuluva and then moved to Kagando Hospital to continue in service until retiring
Robert and Liz Dungel	1972	AIM UK; Builder at Kuluva
Dr Jim McHardy	1973-1976	AIM UK; Doctor at Kuluva
Young Soon	1983-1987	Korean nurse; seconded to AIM from World Concern; first Korean AIM worker to be sent to Africa
Gordon and Grace McCullough	1984-1988	Returned to Uganda with AIM UK; served at Kuluva as hospital administrator and supply officer before moving to Lubowa in Kampala as Branch Exec Officer for AIM
Dr Dick and Sally Ayres	1984-1989	AIM UK; worked with leprosy patients at Kuluva and moved to Leprosy Mission
Dr David and Rebecca Morton	1985-1989	AIM UK then World Concern ; he worked as the Medical Superintendent of the hospital after Dr. Johnson Lulua
Michael Knights	1980s-1990s	AIM UK; he was a Pharmacist at Kuluva Hospital
Brice Crawford	1980s-1990s	AIM USA: volunteer; two years at Kuluva as a male nurse
Andrew Moody	1980s - now	AIM UK; pharmacist; married Eunice, who is Korean from World Concern; both moved to Goli from Kuluva.
Sister Kim	1985- now	AIM USA; seconded to AIM from World Concern for nursing at Kuluva, and Nurse Training School, now at Goli in Nebbi Diocese
Mr Jeff and Mrs Bowman	1980s	Nursing at Kuluva
Audry Lim	1980s	Australian AIM; taught at Ringili
Lisa Lim	1989	AIM USA; Nurse at Kuluva
Molly Coventry	1990s	Volunteer nurse with AIM
Isobel Kempsell	1990s	Volunteer nurse with AIM
Sr. Kim Eun Hee	1990s	Nurse in Kuluva Hospital
Sr. Oh Sun Young	1990s	Nurse in Kuluva Hospital
Sr. Lim Jung Mee	1990s	Nurse in Kuluva Hospital
Sr. Kim Mee Sook	1990s	Nurse in Kuluva Hospital

Sr. Lee Hannah	1990s	Nurse in Kuluva Hospital
Kathleen Burns	1998-2000	AIM UK; Nurse at Kuluva; moved to the Ssese Islands to do work with HIV patients and health education

Missionaries sent by the German Medical Missionary Team (GMMT)		
Werner Wigger Irmela Wigger nee Klohn	1982-2007 1986-2007	Founder of GMMT, both doctors, sending and supporting GMMT missionaries to Kuluva Hospital
Judith Finkbeiner	2000-2001	Nurse at Kuluva Hospital; had to close down the GMMT house due to circumstances at the time; had to leave
Mirko Kloppstech	2005-2006	GMMT Missionaries to Kuluva Hospital; served during the most difficult time in Kuluva
Judith Kloppstech	2005-2006	GMMT Missionaries to Kuluva Hospital; served during the most difficult time in Kuluva
Matthias Muench	1996-1997	Engineer. planned a telephone and loudspeaker system within Kuluva Hospital compound
Esther Muench	1996-1997	Nutritionist; worked in NutritionalUnit at Kuluva hospital.
Dorothee Stamm Hermann Stamm	1987 1987	Medical Doctor Carpenter
Gudrun Jael Schemel	1999	Medical Student
Christine Fritz	1995-1996	Paediatric Nurse; wrote that 'the international community of Kuluva was a blessing to my life'.
Monika Frey	1998-1999 2007-2008	Medical student Paediatrician.
Elke Schullermann	1985-	Worked in the Feeding centre; researched ways to improve the teaching
Christine and Stefan Bösner	1992-1993	Social worker and Deacon in Ringili and medical student. They said, "The time in Uganda was a special time"
Birgit Klumpp	1986-1987, 1989	Kuluva Hospital as Nurse with GMMT; then at Kei PHC

Christliche Fachkraefte International (CFI)	Dates	Remarks (CFI: also CSI Christian Services International)
Wolfgang and Birgit Schäfer	18.05.1987 to 31.05.1990	CoU (Madi West Nile Diocese); architect for re-building Kuluva Hospital; nurse for training nursing staff

Andreas Meck	01.03.1988 to 30.09.1988	CoU (Madi West Nile Diocese), Carpentry training, Kuluva Hospital
Michael and Manuela Auth	September 1988 to July 1991	CoU (Madi West Nile Diocese), Carpentry training and carpentry work for the re-building of Kuluva Hospital
Albert and Erika Feisel	01.09.1990 to 31.10.1999	CoU (Madi West Nile Diocese), Building work, Kuluva Hospital
Dr. Markus and Elke Müller	September 1998 to July 1999	CoU (Madi West Nile Diocese), Doctor at Kuluva Hospital
Dr. Stefan and Carmen Kliebisch	31.05.1999 to 31.05.2001	CoU (Madi West Nile Diocese), Doctor at Kuluva Hospital
Birgit Klumpp	15.02.2001 to 28.02.2007	Here is Life, Community Based Health Care
Daniel Kropf	01.01.2001 to 31.10.2001	Here is Life, Agriculture
Dr. Karl-Friedrich and Beate Neudeck	07.06.1995 to 31.08.2001	CoU (Madi West Nile Diocese), Doctor at Kuluva Hospital
Carola Voigt	18.01.2004 to 31.08.2004	Here is Life, Agriculture
Short-term helpers 1990-1998 : Nadja El-Sawaf, Rebekka Frick, Annalie Rothe, Lydia Vranic, Charlotte Kobler, Anne Rüggemeier, Mirjam Müller		

Appendix 2: Ugandan Clergy ordained in Madi and West Nile Diocese and Nebbi Dioceses

Since the ordination of Silvanus Wani and John H. Droni in 1943, a total of 480 Ugandan clergy have been ordained in the two Dioceses that together form West Nile. The story of the growth in ordinations over the past one hundred years is astonishing, as God has called men and women to the ordained ministry of the Anglican Church in the two Dioceses. The total ordinations in each decade are set out in the table below:

The Growth in Ugandan Clergy West Nile

Decade	Number of Priests ordained
1940s	5
1950s	8
1960s	37
1970s	59
1980s	84
1990s	91
2000s	107
2010s to date	89+

Even in the most difficult years for West Nile, in the 1980s and 1990s, when so many of the Christians had to flee for their lives to find refuge in the Congo, or in very remote areas of the region, men and women responded to God's call to serve His Church. They continue to respond to that call today, and the two Dioceses continue to train and ordain them to serve in both Madi and West Nile and Nebbi Dioceses.

We have listed below priests who were ordained in the Madi West Nile Diocese, and in the Nebbi Diocese, in the first fifty years, up to the year 1968. It would be good to list all the ordained clergy in both Dioceses, but we have run out of space in this book. May the Glory go to our Lord God!

The List of Clergy who worked and are working in West Nile Region

No.	Name	Year of Ordination
Priests from Madi and West Nile Diocese		
1.	Silvanus Wani	1943
2.	John N. Droni	1943
3.	Benon Obetia	1946
4.	Hezekia Ajule	1949
5.	Levi Rukua	1949
6.	Elija Angulibo	1951
7.	Sila Adroa	1955
8.	Matia Magara	1959
9.	Elikana Ondoa	1959
10.	Aroni Dravu	1959
11.	Remelia Ringtho	1962
12.	Timoteo Enima	1962
13.	Yonasani Abukaya	1962
14.	Justo Ocatre	1962
15.	Matia Anguandia	1965
16.	James Baka	1965
17.	Nason Amanzu	1965
18.	Enoka Yada	1965
19.	Hezekia Edoni	1965
20.	Stanley Ozimati	1965
21.	Tefilo Ejiva	1965
22.	Stefano Dralea	1966
23.	Peter Alemiga	1966
24.	Samson Karube	1966
25.	Hilkia Ubia	1967
26.	Erasto A'ia	1968
27.	Paulo Nigo	1968
Priests from Nebbi Diocese		
1.	Hosea Wacibra	1951
2.	Apollo Ukech	1951
3.	James Awor	1959
4.	Efraim Adokutho Nyingwa	1962
5.	Cleopa Ucaya	1965
6.	Joram Ukoku	1965
7.	Simeon Cwinyaai	1966
8.	Andrea Ola	1966
9.	Charles Upoka	1967
10.	Yotam Udeba	1967

People Index

Adroa, Ven Silas T   65
Ajule, Ven Kezekiah   61
Andaku, Bishop Charles   6, 97
Adrale, Bishop Ephraim   89
Anguli'bo, Can. Elijah   67
Anguyo, Can Isaac J   134
Barr, Laura Belle   35
Booth, Rev Bob and Mrs   130
Cole, Stuart Sen. and Mrs   31
Cole, Stuart and May   31
Debo, Tefolo   110
Draku, Archdeacon G   186
Draku, Rev. Can Semi   71
Dravu, Rev Can Aaron A   68
Drati, Bishop Enock   93
Dronyi, Ven John N   64
Enima, Can Timoteo   72
Enyaru, Rev Peninah   22
Gardner, Frank and Edith   21
Grindey, Joy   41
Hooya, John and Ihla   43
Kim, Sister   166
Klumpp, Birgit   45

Kule, Rev Erimayo   74
Lacey, Rev Allan and Anne   52
Lee, Bishop Drati   93
Lloyd, Margaret   40
Luwum, Archbishop Janani   87
Maclure, Rev Seton and Peggy   33
Mawa, Bishop Caleb   91
Moore, Maureen   39
Obetia, Rev Benoni   61
Ofuta, Rev Can Capt Manoa   75, 78
Orombi, Archbishop Henry   4, 99
Payne, Betty and David   75
Ringtho, Bishop Remelia   86
Sarua, Yoram   114
Sharland, David and Heather   25, 162
Taylor, Alastair and Sheila   49
Vollor, Canon and Mrs   26
Waddell, Dr Keith   39
Wani, Bishop Silvanus   83
Wathokodi, Bishop Alphonse   107
Wigger, Dr Werner and Irmela   45
Williams, Dr Peter and Elsie   38
Williams, Dr Ted and Muriel   37